What You Can Do With a

Science

Degree

**OPPORTUNITIES FOR CANADIANS
IN A GLOBAL ECONOMY**

What You Can Do With a Science Degree

OPPORTUNITIES FOR CANADIANS
IN A GLOBAL ECONOMY

Dave Redekopp
Allison Betton
Mary Munro

Trifolium Books Inc.
Toronto

Published by arrangement with Hobsons Publishing PLC.

Canadian Cataloguing in Publication Data
Redekopp, David, E.D. (David Eric Dean), 1960-
    What you can do with a science degree : opportunities for Canadians in a global economy

ISBN 1-895579-96-1

1. Science - Vocational guidance - Canada. I. Betton, Allison, 1970-   . II. Munro, Mary 1938-   .
III. Title.

Q149.C3R42 1997   502.371   C97-930897-6

Printed and bound in Canada
10 9 8 7 6 5 4 3 2 1

Cover and text design: Rick Eskins

Ordering Information
Orders by bookstores, wholesalers, individuals, organizations, and educational institutions: Please contact General Distribution Services, 34 Lesmill Road, Don Mills, Ontario, Canada M3B 2T6; tel. Ontario and Quebec (800) 387-0141, all other provinces (800) 387-0172; fax (416) 445-5967. In the U.S.A., contact General Distribution Services, 85 River Rock Road, Suite 202, Buffalo, NY 14207; tel. 1-800-805-1083; fax (416) 445-5967.

Trifolium's books may also be purchased in bulk for educational, business, or promotional use. For information please telephone (416) 925-0765 or write: Special Sales, Trifolium Books Inc., 238 Davenport Road, Suite 28, Toronto, Ontario, M5R 1J6

CONTENTS

INTRODUCTION

Science is a part of virtually all areas of modern life. Whether it's in the formulation of new ideas, the refinement of knowledge, the development of new products, a concern for the environment, an understanding of crucial issues of health and safety, or a straightforward curiosity about why things are the way they are and how they work, science touches us all.

Between 1991 and 1994, the number of students graduating from Canadian universities with degrees in science and science-related disciplines increased by nearly 10,000. Today, the numbers are even higher. More and more students appear to be looking to the sciences for their degrees.

Many science graduates use their degree as a stepping stone to careers inside, as well as outside, science. In fact, science graduates can enter most fields that other graduates do, and many more. They can consider job areas where a science degree is required, as well as careers where any degree is acceptable.

Most careers for science graduates fall into three main groupings:

1. careers that rely on specialist scientific knowledge;

2. careers using generalist scientific knowledge, as well as other qualities or skills;

3. careers using other aspects of your science education; for example, transferable skills such as problem solving, numeracy, and teamwork skills. (For more on transferable skills and their importance, see Chapter 3.)

Science graduates typically find employment from these three groups at different stages of their careers. In today's world of work, career paths are seldom linear. For example, in the past, a degree in a subject area usually led to a position with advancement within the same organization, institution, or company. More often than not, a person stayed within that same framework — both the employer and the job structure — for one's entire working life. Not so today, the diverse careers our world now includes may initially seem "mind-boggling" but do, nevertheless, afford tremendous opportunities to explore a variety of careers in a single lifetime.

Changes and Choices

Over the next few years, we will continue to see substantial changes in the world of work. Some jobs will disappear, but new opportunities will also arise. There are many factors influencing these changes, from government downsizing to the concern for the environment. While federal and provincial governments may have fewer full-time employees, there has been a notable increase in the number of people hired as consultants or contractors (more on these work alternatives in Chapter 7). For example, in recent government downsizing, an acoustical engineer for the Department of Defense, who is known by one of the authors, lost his position. He almost immediately was contracted by the Ministry of the Environment to put his talents and skills to use to help establish programs to track whale populations. Similar changes are occurring in the private sector; just look at the increase in small and home-based business. Trends like these will affect prospects for science graduates so it is important to know about them.

You will change, too. You will develop new skills and interests. And you may discover that you are much better than you thought at some of the things you find difficult now.

Your priorities will also change. You may find, for example, that you become passionately involved in an environmental issue and need a knowledge of chemistry to understand the problem or contribute to a solution. Or perhaps the factors that lured you into a particular career — such as a good starting salary — may lose their lustre after the first few years of work.

Will the choices you make now seem worthwhile several years down the road? Will you be able to progress in the career path you chart for yourself? Will you have the right skills to help you move along that path, or onto another one if you decide to change direction?

The more information and advice you can get about your options now, the more chance there is that you will make decisions — about courses and careers — that will be satisfying.

If you are a high school student making decisions about which science courses to take and wondering how your choices will affect future opportunities, you'll find the first two chapters of this book especially helpful. Chapter 1 discusses the value of studying science and common concerns about science. Chapter 2 describes the connections between high school and post-secondary science courses. This chapter will help you to see which doors you are opening, or closing, by choosing certain science courses and eliminating others.

If you are thinking about or have already begun your degree program, you will find the information in the rest of the book useful in your exploration of the opportunities available to science students and graduates. Chapters 3 through 6 describe a range of options such as finding work after graduation, graduate and post-graduate programs, and gaining international experience. Chapters 7 and 8 discuss the work alternatives emerging from the changing workplace and career building for science graduates. These chapters will help you to imagine your preferred future and to find ways to work toward that future.

This book will help you see the links between science subjects and the wide range of employment opportunities open to science graduates. Equally important, this book will help you recognize and ask the right questions of yourself and of other people. It's a starting point for your decisions about where science can take you in the 21st century.

ONE

THE VALUE OF STUDYING SCIENCE

If you've picked up this book, you probably want to find out where your interest in or aptitude for science can take you in the years ahead. And you're not alone. You're part of a growing number of people who are recognizing the value of studying for a science degree as part of their aspirations to find and secure employment.

It wasn't always this way. According to a Statistics Canada bulletin published in 1989, less than 15% of high school graduates pursued studies in science-related areas such as agriculture, biology, chemistry, engineering, geology, health professions, mathematics, or physics. What a difference a decade makes! Today, more students than ever before are taking science degrees.

Why the increase? One reason is that the world of work has undergone dramatic changes in recent years. The biggest change is in *how* work is being done — from predominantly full-time employment to work alternatives such as contracting and consulting. In previous years, companies often paid employees whether all their time was productive or not. Now, in a global marketplace, companies have to be competitive. It may be more efficient to hire someone to complete a particular task or project, rather than as a full-time employee. Developments in communication technologies have facilitated this transition. There is still a lot of "work" to do; it just isn't packaged as a "job" as often. As a science graduate, you are ideally positioned to take advantage of these opportunities. There is an increasing demand for scientific and technological expertise in many sectors of the economy including energy and natural resources, the environment, logistics, medical sciences, and computer sciences, just to name a few. You could consult on several projects at once, take on a full-time contract position for a set period of time, or become an entrepreneur offering services or products to clients. (Remember the underwater acoustic engineer from the Introduction?)

Another reason for the increase in students taking science degrees is that science graduates can enter nearly all the job areas that arts graduates go into, particularly if they have good communication skills. But they have the added advantage of being able to use their subject knowledge in a variety of ways, either directly or indirectly, in a host of job areas that are closed to non-science graduates.

However, even with this optimistic outlook, many students dismiss science as a possible degree option because of some particularly ingrained misconceptions and half-truths. These require closer examination.

Is Science Difficult?

In a survey of Alberta high school students, strong criticism was directed at chemistry and physics studies. Students found chemistry irrelevant, stating they could find no way to connect the subject to "real life." Physics, meanwhile, was a source of terror; when asked to explain further, students described physics as "math, super-hard math."

Interestingly, despite their criticisms, the same students felt that science is an important part of high school education, and most were taking at least two science subjects. And for one subject in particular, Grade 12 biology, there was unanimous agreement that it is the most important senior course.

So, clearly, science is considered valuable. But is it difficult? The most honest answer is: "That depends."

Certainly, some sciences are seen more challenging than others. Biology, for example, has a reputation for being the "easiest" of the sciences. Maybe that's because students can more readily see the applications of biology concepts to "real life." Perhaps also the math component that plays such an important role in physics and, to a lesser degree, chemistry is less evident in high school biology classes. And yes, people who enjoy biology and do very well in it often are less confident in math.

However, everyone is different in the way they approach and understand different subjects. Unfortunately, when students come up against concepts they have trouble understanding, or skills they have trouble applying, they often get discouraged — sometimes so much so that they come to believe they can't, or won't, ever succeed.

This may sound trite, but it's nevertheless true: Nearly all people have difficulties with certain subjects at some stage of their lives. (Yes, there are a few "whiz kids," but they are an extremely small minority.) Most of the time, what's needed is extra effort to get back on track.

If you feel that at any time you are falling behind, it is vital to ask for help and support immediately, because it can be difficult to recover if you leave the problem unresolved for too long.

An experienced math teacher's advice to students

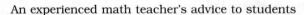

What Can You Do If You Need Help?

☞ Seek advice from your teacher (or professor, if you're already in university).

☞ Find an experienced tutor. (Talk to other students; word-of-mouth is usually the best source of information about which tutors to contact and ones to avoid.)

☞ Switch to another class, if possible. (This is usually more common at university than secondary school.)

☞ Most importantly, avoid the temptation to label yourself as "dumb" or "a failure." In the vast majority of situations, difficulties

in learning new ideas and skills are overcome through renewed effort, a willingness
to persevere, and — above all — patience.

Does a Science Degree Guarantee a Job?

No — no degree can do that. But it can give you a clear advantage by opening up a broader range of career options than
an arts degree. Studying for a degree in accounting or law
may seem safer or more likely to result in employment, but if
you really like science and want to give yourself more flexibility in your career plans, science is an excellent choice to
make. The important thing is to gather as much information
as you can before making your decisions.

Does Studying Science Mean Having to Become a Scientist?

Many people seem to confuse science as a subject with science as a career. This isn't the case with other subjects people
study. For example, few students of French imagine themselves as French teachers or interpreters; those who study
history are seldom planning to become historians.

Many people choose subjects to study because they're interested in them or good at them, not necessarily because
they might lead to a particular career. Why should it be any
different with science?

So, no — studying science doesn't mean you have to become a scientist. Nor does it mean you'll be limited to a career
as a researcher. Many science students take research positions, but that's usually because they choose to, not because
that's all there is available to them. More than half of all graduate vacancies, including those outside of science, will be
open to successful science graduates.

But Science Is for Nerds, Right?

It's a powerful caricature: the image of the scientist sporting
a white lab coat and pop-bottle glasses, with poor hygiene and

strange hair. And don't forget: he (it's always a man) has a leaky pen in his top pocket, mumbles to himself, talks with a nasally voice, and — well, he's just plain dull, isn't he?

The media play a major role in promoting this distorted image of the scientist, and science people in general. But it is a distortion. For every scientist who actually fits the caricature (and, let's face it, there are a few "nerds" in science, just as there are a few "nerds" in law, journalism, business, and every other profession), there are many thousands more who don't. [And, what's more, just what is a "nerd?"]

The people who choose to study science do it for some very practical reasons: they find it interesting and enjoyable; they've gotten good marks in the subject in earlier grades; they need the subject as a prerequisite for further studies; and they recognize its value for future employment opportunities.

Science Is a Man's Field, Isn't It?

Historically, this has certainly been true. Even though there have been women active in science for thousands of years, their contributions have been largely ignored or "taken over" by men. For example, one of the most widely read early medical texts in Europe was written by an Italian woman named Trotula. She was one of a group of medical women dubbed the "Ladies of Salerno." Over the years, however, her name had been removed from the text and it came to be assumed that it was written by a man.

Today, the situation for women has very much changed for the better. More and more women are pursuing careers in science, especially in areas that have long discouraged women such as applied sciences and engineering. In fact, according to the Canadian Council of Professional Engineers, the number of women with undergraduate degrees in engineering rose from 881 in 1991 to 1,363 in 1995 — an increase of nearly 65%. This activity is supported by the work of organizations such as Women in Science and Engineering (WISE), a national group with local branches that provides courses and speakers to counsel female students who are interested in (or anxious about pursuing) science.

Young Science Graduates Tell Their Stories

There are plenty of good reasons for considering doing a science degree. Throughout this book, you will find profiles of young science graduates explaining the courses they took and their effect on the work they do now. Here's some initial advice from some of these graduates.

Karen Farrant
(chemistry-with-French graduate; now a Ph.D. student in France)
"Studying science has many bonuses. One particular advantage for me is that it helped me get summer jobs. This has helped me financially all the way through my degree."

Stephen Walton
(natural sciences graduate; now a patent agent)
"What I like about the work I do is the challenge and variety. It's exciting, but it's vital to be precise and methodical. My science background gave me an ideal background."

Mairi Macdonald
(physics graduate; now a senior official at a telecommunications company)
"Too often, people underestimate themselves. My mother always says she doesn't understand science, but I'm no smarter than she is. She could easily understand it if she wanted to. What she lacks is the motivation to do it."

Rick Duncan
(chemistry graduate; now in marketing with Shell)
"I've seen too many of my friends wind up regretting dropping out of science by the middle of high school. Stick with science as long as you can, even if you aren't sure where it'll take you. Why lock doors before you even know which ones you might want to open later?"

TWO

CHOOSING YOUR DEGREE PROGRAM

This chapter covers:

- ⊃ The variety of science courses available;
- ⊃ The links between science courses in high school and degree courses;
- ⊃ The importance of mathematics;
- ⊃ How you can keep open a range of options;
- ⊃ Where to go for further information and advice.

Things to Think About

There are a number of questions you can ask yourself to help you decide on your degree program. For example:

- ⊃ Do I want to build on the science subjects I'm taking at present and look at programs where these courses are requirements for entry?

- ⊃ Shall I look at programs where some scientific knowledge and interest is required, but which take people with a wide range of backgrounds?

- ⊃ Should I consider programs which will accept students with any high school science subjects?

You'll also need to consider different levels of study, whether you want a degree or diploma, and how full-time courses compare with co-op courses. Would you rather study a single subject or do a combined program? Have you thought of spending any time getting work experience as part of your studies? What about studying in another country as part of your program? These are a few of the many questions you need to ask yourself. It's your future. Only you can make the choice that's right for you.

In Canada, undergraduate degree programs are three or four years long. Co-op programs last four or five years, where periods of full-time study alternate with periods of practical experience in a working situation. Diploma courses are often different in approach from degree courses and may include more project-based work. Most diploma programs last two years, and are offered at community colleges and institutes of technology.

The minimum requirement for most degree courses is a high school diploma with five grade 12 subjects, one of which must be English. However, requirements vary among universities and colleges, so if you are applying to a university in another province, be sure to check the equivalents to your province's high school courses.

Degree Subjects

Subject titles don't always give a clear idea of what the courses are about. Make a list of the ones that interest you and find out more about them. The glossary beginning on page 89 will help here. You'll find other useful sources of information in the Resource List on pages 115-117.

Courses that Require High School Sciences

First, there are courses in subjects you are very familiar with from high school — the basic sciences: biology, chemistry, physics, and mathematics. Then there are science subjects you might have come across at high school, but perhaps did not study in detail. Some examples include geology (or earth sciences), environmental science, computer science, and psychology. In addition, there are many courses offering combinations of these subjects, as well as these subjects together with a variety of different ones.

The next few pages provide an overview of the range of study opportunities available to you. They have been categorized as follows:

1 More specialist science subjects, some of which you may have touched on at secondary school

2 The "main" engineering subjects

3 The specialist engineering subjects

4 Medically-related courses (which also lead to professional qualifications)

5 Courses relating to agriculture, environmental, and conservation sciences

6 Courses for which some science knowledge is useful or required.

Keep in mind that these lists are not fully comprehensive, although they do cover most subject areas. New subject combinations and new courses with new titles appear every year. You'll need the most up-to-date information before you make your choice.

1   More Specialist Science Subjects

Acoustics	Geochemistry
Anatomy	Geography (B.Sc.)
Artificial intelligence	Geology
Astronomy	Geophysics
Astrophysics	Immunology
Bacteriology	Marine biology
Biochemistry	Materials science
Biophysics	Metallurgy
Biotechnology	Microbiology
Botany	Molecular biology

Computer science
Cybernetics
Earth sciences
Ecology
Electronics
Environmental science
Ergonomics
Food science
Forensic science
Genetics

Nutrition
Oceanography
Parasitology
Pathology
Pharmacology
Physiology
Polymer science
Statistics
Virology
Zoology

These subjects can often be taken in combination with a basic science subject or with each other. They could even be studied together with a completely different subject such as marketing, a foreign language, or business studies.

2   The "Main" Engineering Subjects

Chemical engineering
Civil engineering

Electrical engineering
Mechanical engineering

All engineering subjects require math and physics.

3   The Specialist Engineering Subjects

Acoustical engineering
Aeronautical engineering
Aerospace systems
   engineering
Agricultural engineering
Air transport engineering
Automotive engineering
Biochemical engineering
Computer engineering
Control engineering
Design engineering
Energy engineering
Environmental engineering

Marine engineering
Metallurgical engineering
Mining engineering
Naval architecture
Nuclear engineering
Petroleum engineering
Plant engineering
Power engineering
Structural engineering
Systems engineering
Telecommunications
   engineering

For this group of specialist courses, you really do have to find out if the course is what you think it will be and make sure you investigate the employment prospects thoroughly. This is particularly important because specialist courses like these are usually aimed at employment in a very specific industry, and are less likely to be directly applicable to a wide range of other jobs.

4   Medically-related Courses

Chiropody/podiatry
Dentistry
Dietetics/Nutrition
Environmental health
Medicine
Midwifery
Nursing
Occupational therapy
Ophthalmic optics

Optometry
Orthoptics
Pharmacy
Physiotherapy
Radiography
Respiratory therapy
Speech therapy
Veterinary science

Courses in both medicine and veterinary science will include many of the subjects listed on page 17, such as anatomy, physiology, biochemistry, pharmacology, and pathology, in addition to clinical studies. Other less traditional North American areas such as chiropractic medicine, naturopathy, and homeopathy also today afford career opportunities.

5   Courses Relating to Agriculture, Environmental, and Conservation Sciences

Agriculture
Animal science
Arboriculture
Conservation biology
Crop science
Fishery science
Forest management
Forest resources

Horticulture
Land remediation and
   reclamation
Land resource science
Wildlife and rangeland
   conservation
Wildlife restoration

6   Courses for which Some Science Knowledge Is Useful or Required

Anthropology (physical)
Archaeology
Architecture
Behavioural sciences
Cartography
Computer studies
History of science
Information science
Kinesiology
Landscape architecture

Linguistics and speech
   therapy
Nursing
Occupational therapy
Photography
Physiotherapy
Psychology
Recreation studies
Town and country planning
Urban & regional planning

Looking at Your Range of Options from a New Angle

Here's another way of considering the subjects that might interest you in higher education. Start with your favourite basic science subject and see what the option lists look like.

Is Your Favourite Subject Mathematics?

If so, the following courses might appeal to you:

Actuarial science
Aeronautical engineering (P)
Aerospace systems (P)
Agricultural engineering (P)
Artificial intelligence
Astronomy (P)
Chemical engineering (P)
Civil engineering (P)
Computer science
Control engineering (P)
Cybernetics
Electrical engineering (P)
Electronics (P)

Management science
Materials science (P)
Mathematical engineering (P)
Mathematics
Mechanical engineering (P)
Meteorology (P)
Naval architecture (P)
Nuclear engineering (P)
Operational research
Physics (P)
Software engineering
Statistics

(P) means you will probably require two years of high school physics or equivalent to take these subjects.

Is Your Favourite Subject Physics?

If so, these subjects might suit you:

Acoustical engineering (M)
Aeronautical engineering (M)
Aerospace systems (M)
Agricultural engineering (M)
Astronomy (M)
Astrophysics (M)
Biomedical engineering (M)
Biophysics (M)
Chemical engineering (M)
Civil engineering (M)
Computer science
Control engineering (M)
Cybernetics
Dentistry
Design engineering (M)
Earth sciences (M)
Electrical engineering (M)
Electronics (M)
Environmental
    engineering/science (M)
Ergonomics
Geology
Geophysics (M)
Materials science (M)
Mathematical engineering (M)
Mathematics (M)
Mechanical engineering (M)
Medical physics
Meteorology (M)
Naval architecture (M)
Nuclear engineering (M)
Oceanography
Optics/optical sciences
Orthoptics
Photography
Physics (M)
Physiotherapy
Polymer science
Quantity surveying
Software engineering
Statistics

(M) means you will probably need grade 12 mathematics or equivalent to take these subjects.

Is Your Favourite Subject Chemistry?

If so, you might like to consider these subjects:

Biochemistry (S)
Biology (S)
Biomedical science (S)
Biotechnology (S)
Chemical engineering (P)
Chemistry (S)
Crystallography
Dietetics (S)
Ecology (S)
Medicine (S)
Metallurgy (P)
Microbiology (S)
Minerals engineering (P)
Molecular biology
Nutrition(S)
Paper sciences (S)
Pathology (S)
Pharmacology (S)

Environmental health
Food science (S)
Geochemistry (P)
Immunology (S)
Materials science (P)
Medical laboratory
    sciences (S)

Pharmacy (S)
Photographic sciences (S)
Physiology (S)
Polymer science (P)

(P) means you will probably need to have two years of physics or equivalent.

(S) means you will need at least one other grade 12 science subject.

Is Your Favourite Subject Biology?

If so, the following subjects might appeal:

Agriculture
Anatomy (C)
Anthropology
Arboriculture
Bacteriology (C)
Biochemistry (C)
Biology (C)
Biomedical science (C)
Biotechnology (C)
Botany (C)
Chiropody
Chiropractic
Dentistry (C)
Dietetics (C)
Ecology (C)
Environmental health
Food science (C)
Forestry (C)
Genetics (C)
Horticulture
Immunology (C)

Landscape architecture
Marine biology
Medical laboratory
    sciences (C)
Medicine (C)
Microbiology
Nutrition (C)
Occupational therapy
Oceanography
Ophthalmic optics
Orthoptics
Parasitology (C)
Pathology (C)
Pharmacology (C)
Physiology (C)
Physiotherapy
Psychology
Speech therapy
Sports studies
Veterinary science (C)
Zoology (C)

(C) means you will need grade 12 chemistry or equivalent to take these subjects.

Another Angle for Examining Your Options

Yet another approach might be helpful. Consider again the four basic subjects needed to pursue a science degree: biology, chemistry, physics, and math. For the widest possible choice of courses in higher education, you need all four. If this isn't feasible (or desirable), your options do narrow a bit. Here are the consequences.

No Mathematics?

This would eliminate courses and careers in math, physics, engineering, and technology. Math is also useful to support most of the other sciences and would be helpful for other degree courses such as economics and management sciences.

If you are quite sure you don't want to go into the more mathematical areas and feel that your interests lie more on the biological and biochemical side, then you will probably need fewer math courses than for pursuits in the physical sciences. On other hand, if you find out that you need mathematics later on, keep in mind that most people find it easier to pick up biology on their own than to make up lost ground in math.

No Physics?

This would limit your choice of courses and careers in physics, engineering, and technology, and would cut your range in mathematics. There are other careers such as optics, acoustics, and meteorology where physics is involved. If you want to do biological or chemical subjects, then physics may not be so badly missed, particularly if you have taken applied mathematics. However, physics does support chemistry and would help you with the molecular aspects of biology.

No Chemistry?

If this leaves you with both math and physics, you still have the whole range of mathematical, physics, and engineering careers to choose from. However, without chemistry, you would be disadvantaged in fields such as chemical engineering and other biological and biochemical subjects for which chemistry is more important than biology. Dropping chemistry is a mistake if you are interested in medicine, veterinary science, or pharmacy.

No Biology?

While biology is the most popular high school science course, it's usually regarded as the least "hard" of the sciences. What this means is unclear. Possibly it's because biology is a more descriptive science and many people find the concepts easier to grasp than those in physics. But this is changing as the study of biology delves deeper into what goes on at the molecular and cellular levels. As mentioned a few moments ago, most people find it easier to study biology on their own and catch up with the subject later on, say at university, than if they had missed out on other basic sciences. Biology is very rarely a specific requirement for entry to degree courses (even for biology!), although it counts fully as a science subject if the entry requirement is for two unspecified science subjects.

People who are interested in a biology-related career often include biology in their science course choices because it seems more relevant than the other basic sciences to their ultimate goal — say, medicine or agriculture. If you think you might want to study biological subjects in university, you don't require high school biology as a prerequisite. However, make sure you *do* have chemistry, because it will be essential for first-year university biology courses.

What If You Have Only One or Two Basic Sciences?

Many secondary students take only two or even one of the basic science subjects in grade 12. This is often because they want to include a wider range of subjects such as language courses in their programs.

Having just one or two basic sciences will clearly narrow your choices for higher education, but this won't matter if the careers and further courses being eliminated aren't of any interest to you. For example, a combination of math, physics, and social studies leaves open a wide range of math, physics, and engineering options, but cuts out courses requiring chemistry (such as medicine and biochemistry). A choice of chemistry, biology, and French would make it difficult to get into engineering and physics-related careers as well as those requiring a high level of mathematics.

Karen Farrant (see page 59) took only mathematics and chemistry in grade 12. She is now doing research in a biological area even though she did not study biology.

The best way of reviewing the career options leading from any particular choice of two basic sciences is to look at the careers and further courses being eliminated, or made less direct to enter, by the combination you are considering. You can use the lists above to help you. It's also important to check the entry requirements of the specific programs or faculties you are interested in. Many require a minimum of two grade 12 sciences *and* grade 12 math.

What About Just One Basic Science?

It's usually not a good idea to take either physics or chemistry on its own, unless you are just interested in widening your choice for general educational reasons rather than studying sciences beyond high school. The most usual single subjects are mathematics (which is useful for economics and business courses) and biology (which is a good foundation for paramedical studies or for those who might find it useful later on, in elementary school teaching, for example). However, a single science course is really too narrow a base for most science degrees.

What Grades Will You Need?

Choosing subjects on the basis of grades required, rather than on following your scientific and career interests, isn't likely to end in success. However, it is also sensible to be realistic: in some courses, such as medicine and veterinary sciences, the competition is such that high grades are needed to get in.

Very often the grades required for a degree program depend more on the popularity of the course than on the difficulty of the subject. So there are huge variations between universities and colleges in terms of the grades they require for the same subject, as well as for different subjects. There are exceptions, however. Although mathematics and physics, for example, have never had a very high ratio of applicants to places, these courses tend to attract students with high grades. This is possibly because most students feel these subjects would be too difficult, or because they have been advised against doing them.

Information about the minimum grades required for degree programs is published in the university calendars. Remember, this information may help you to look at your applications realistically, but should not be used as the sole basis for your choice. As universities take more students, the required grades have been dropping a little. Many colleges have less stringent entrance requirements such as only four grade 12 subjects or a combination of grade 11 and grade 12 subjects.

Where Can You Find Help If You Need It?

Help in identifying your scientific interests?

⊃   Try a careers interest questionnaire.

⊃   Talk to your science teachers.

⊃   Read more about the subjects in university calendars and guides to higher education.

⊃   Widen your general science knowledge through magazines such as *Equinox* or *Scientific American*; the science pages of newspapers; "popular" science books, and biographies; TV and radio programs; and "taster" courses at universities.

Help in fitting courses to your interests?

⊃   Try an interactive computer program such as CHOICES or *Discover*.

⊃   Talk to your science teachers.

⊃   Talk to your career officer or guidance counsellor.

⊃   Consult reference books and others in the Resource List (page 115).

Help in finding out what particular courses will cover?

⊃   Send for calendars from universities.

⊃   Visit higher education establishments, or go to open houses.

⊃   If possible, talk to someone who has taken the course.

⊃   Consult reference books and others in the Resource List (page 115).

Help in looking at careers with a science degree?

⊃   Read the rest of this book and follow further references that interest you.

⊃   Use your school's or community's career library.

⊃   Ask local employers.

⊃   Talk to your career officer or guidance counsellor.

⊃   Try some work experience or summer jobs.

⊃   Discuss your thoughts with family and friends.

⊃   Speak with people in the field who are doing the kind of work you're interested in (do a so-called "Information Interview").

A Final Word

This chapter is just a starting point. There are many other things to be done before you can reach a decision. There are new ideas to consider, people to talk to, and other sources of help and information to explore. New courses are offered every year and all sorts of combinations you will never have heard of that may be available at just one or two institutions. So you must consult the most up-to-date reference. It is important that you find out what the science courses in higher education are about, particularly if they are subjects you haven't experienced in high school. Don't just assume that you know.

Consider the stage you're at now and decide where you are in your career planning. Draw up a plan of action using the suggestions in this book and then add your own. For example, you might want to talk to someone who is already in a job that interests you. The more you find out, the more your interests will clarify and new ideas will grow.

THREE

CHOOSING AND WORKING WITH YOUR SCIENCE DEGREE

This chapter covers:

⊃ Some of the criteria you might employ in choosing a science degree

⊃ The three main ways that people use their science degrees in jobs

⊃ A look at the transferable skills that increase career options for science graduates.

Choosing a Degree Program

Once you've decided which subject or subjects you're interested in studying, you will be faced with another set of choices. What kind of course do you want to follow? For example, you could aim toward a degree in one subject or go for a course which leads to a combined degree, such as science and business studies. There are also co-op (sometimes called "internship") programs available on which you spend a period of time in related work as part of the degree program. You could also choose to take an honours degree program. Students are typically admitted to these programs after one year of study and must maintain a certain overall grade average in order to remain in the program. Honours programs are usually geared toward students who plan to continue on to graduate studies.

To help you with your choices you can get lots of information from school guidance counsellors, career centres in your community, career counsellors, and university career centres. There are also many useful reference materials available. See page 115 for a list of some helpful sources of print and electronic information. You will discover that most degree programs require you to study a variety of subjects at least for the first year, before you specialize.

At some stage you will have to decide how broad you wish your course to be. Do you want to concentrate on one specialist area and build up more in-depth knowledge? This may be with a view to taking your interest further in a job, in research and development, or in studying for a graduate degree. You may, on the other hand, want a wider program which covers all aspects of, say, chemistry or which includes at least two basic science subjects throughout. You might choose a course like materials science or environmental science which calls on a variety of basic sciences in a multi-disciplinary approach to a major topic. There are also some specialized degree courses in subjects like geophysics, paleontology, marine biology, information science, and astronomy, which lead towards very specific job areas.

More or Less Technical: It's Up to You

The direction you take will depend largely on your own interests and how they develop. If you are sure you want your science degree to be part of a general scientific education — a base on which you can build either job training or further qualifications — you won't be disadvantaged by taking a broader degree. In fact, for careers that let you use sciences in a particular work setting, such as teaching, information science, or scientific journalism, it could really be an asset.

If you want to use your science degree in a completely unrelated field, such as one of the financial areas, it won't matter very much which way you go. (Mind you, it's always an advantage to have done well even if you don't want to go on with the academic subject.) Employers are usually more impressed by people who have maintained a good average and who wish to change track than by people who look as if they are doing it because they weren't successful.

Keep in mind that there are dangers in too narrow a specialization. Your interests could take you into a very specific area such as studying fish viruses where there may not be many jobs. On the other hand, you could suddenly become the most sought-after specialist on an unforeseen problem or development. You might strike it lucky, with employers falling over themselves to entice you to work for them. These situations are not easy to predict, but they do happen. For example, in the early 1990s, botanists doing research on various types of pollen never imagined that their skills might suddenly become useful to the oil industry. But when it was found that you could predict the presence of oil from an analysis of the pollen evidence in shales, these scientists were immediately in demand.

Whole new areas of science, such as biotechnology and polymer sciences, continue to emerge and develop as breakthroughs are made in basic research. People are working in these new areas long before they become part of the science courses in universities, so there is a constant reassessment of scientific knowledge and a demand for skills that is very hard to predict.

Janine Pelletier

The science graduate in this profile chose to apply her physics degree in industrial research. She wanted to work for a company where she would not be confined to a lab and where she could make good use of her communication skills.

Career Profile

Age: 27
Senior Professional, Network Research with a telecommunications company
Favourite High School Subjects: math, physics, chemistry, German
Degree: physics with industrial physics (Honours)

Janine chose her grade 12 courses knowing that she wanted to do science, as well as study a second language: German.

The university she attended requires students to study four subjects in the first year and two in the second year. (Janine took math and physics.) She took physics in the third year, and physics with industrial physics in the fourth year.

Janine says she found it a very interesting and challenging course. By the end of the second year she was finding math less interesting but necessary: "a useful tool for physics." The broad first-year course gave her a basic knowledge of most sciences which she finds helps her to communicate with other scientists with different specializations.

At the end of her degree program Janine contemplated doing an M.Sc. but felt she did not have enough drive to push ahead on her own on a particular topic. There was no specific area she felt she wanted to study, so she started looking for opportunities in large companies. She knew she wanted more than research work, and eventually landed a position with a telecommunications company.

Janine is team leader of the "optical interconnects" section, which deals with the optical fibre equivalents of junction boxes and the "optical wiring" in telephone networks. She is responsible for the work of six to ten people. In the lab they put together prototypes and take optical measurements. Much of the design work involves computer modelling. Janine spends about ten percent of her time actually in the lab. She does a lot of reading to keep up with research reports, collating useful information and discussing the direction of the section's work with others. She also keeps an eye on what the company's competitors (mainly in North America and Japan) are doing and keeps non-scientific departments informed of technical developments. It is very important in her job to be able to communicate well and write clear reports.

Satisfactions for Janine: "When an idea comes together for the first time and it works — even if it never gets to be a viable product. I also enjoy the people management and persuading people to take a look at another point of view."

She does not feel disadvantaged in not having a Ph.D. Although there is an option to do one through the company, she doesn't want to commit three years to following the same subject. However, she is doing an M.Sc. course in telecommunications which is run on-site. This is a part-time course with a project. Classes are half in company time and half in the staff's own time. The course fees are paid by the company.

Janine's plans for the future are to stay where she is for about two years, gaining technical and management experience, then to move on either within research (to become head of a group) or into network studies. There has been a recent expansion in the software side and the company needs more technical people.

She feels that she is very well paid, particularly in comparison with her university friends who went into science teaching. Janine's advice to others who are interested in applied research is to maintain as broad a range of sciences as possible unless you want to go for a Ph.D. "The qualities I need for my type of work are strong analytical skills, a broad science background, and good communication skills."

What Do You Want to Do After You Graduate?

Although many people begin university with some career plans, their ideas sometimes change as they find out more about themselves, their subjects, and the career options open to them. Not surprisingly, then, lots of people change their minds about their original choice of courses and about their career aims. Some students have a career in mind from when they are very young, but many others start out with few ideas about what they want to do. In fact, at least half of the students in higher education graduate in subjects other than those they initially applied to study.

Fortunately, most university and college courses are flexible enough to allow for change and development. But the situation varies, so keep this in mind as a factor to look for when choosing a course. This flexibility will help to keep your options open and will give you the chance to experience some new areas before you are fully committed. When you consider possible courses, find out at what point you have to make your final decision on your degree subject or subjects.

Aaron Devoetsky

This profile shows someone who had no idea of what he wanted to do but who found the perfect job through a computer profile and an introduction at a careers fair.

Career Profile

Age: 25
Trainee Patent Agent
Favourite High School Subjects: math, physics, chemistry, French
Degree: natural sciences (final year subjects: molecular and cell biology)

Aaron chose a degree in natural sciences because it allowed him to study a range of different science subjects. He felt this was his best course of action because, "I didn't have a clue what I wanted to do."

He liked the challenge of a course that was very demanding. The workload was heavy, with three experimental subjects in the first two years. This meant three whole days of labs, 12 lectures, and three supervisions (discussions about his work with his supervisor) per week. In his second year he chose biochemistry, molecular biology, and pathology. Three practical projects in his final year gave him a taste of what life in research would be like.

While he was keen to use his science, Aaron decided against a career as a "hands on" scientist. He considered scientific journalism, being unaware of any other options. Many of his friends were going into accounting and management consulting, but these jobs didn't appeal to him, despite the higher starting salaries.

At a careers fair after graduation he met a patent agent; he had learned about the work through a computer-based system he had used at the careers service. (A patent is a form of "permission" that's granted to people for a set length of time to protect their inventions from being copied by others.) A patent agent obtains patents for clients and advises on existing patents. This sometimes means starting at square one with a completely new invention, meeting the inventor, and writing the patent application. On other occasions the work begins further on in the life of a patent application, prosecuting a patent which someone else has written. Aaron deals mainly with patents in biotechnology, but has also drafted applications for many different inventions including a baby bottle, a winch for yachts, and a bathmat.

Aaron says that the key to the work is not high-level scientific expertise so much as the ability to understand technology quickly and the knack of writing a full and clear description of the product or process. A patent application is examined rigorously by the Patent Office and objections are usually raised. During the prosecution of an application before a patent officer, skills of advocacy (putting forward your case) become the main requirement.

Communication with the Patent Office is mostly in writing, but oral hearings are held when necessary. This work can be rather like that of a lawyer, presenting evidence and attempting to answer challenges on the spot. In some cases, Aaron works as part of a team with lawyers.

Day to day, Aaron has to be flexible, moving quickly from one patent problem to another. Some situations demand emergency action and mean rearranging his priorities. There are always deadlines to be met in order to keep a patent application alive. The decisions he makes and the advice he gives daily can have significant repercussions. A great deal of money and many jobs can depend on patents being secure, protecting the investment of companies in the development of their inventions. Advice given by a patent agent will often shape the business plan and determine the investment and marketing strategy of a company.

The satisfactions for Aaron: "What I like about the work is both the challenge and the variety. Each job is different because, by definition, patents are about new ideas. It's exciting, but it's also vital to be precise and methodical. My science degree is an ideal background."

Although Aaron said he was not as well paid as his friends at first (those going into accounting, for instance) his salary has increased rapidly and will continue to do so. When you become a partner - which Aaron hopes for eventually - the rewards are very good.

Using Your Degree

We recommend this begin earlier - even as early as first year. This way, students can do volunteer work and find summer jobs in the field of interest to get a better sense of the "fit." Working in the field is not the same as studying it. Early in your degree program, take stock and consider the options open to you. You can look again at your chosen science subject, or subjects, and decide whether or not you want to continue in more depth. As early as possible and throughout your program, all the different ways you can use your degree in the next stage of your career.

There are three directions you can take:

1. building on your scientific knowledge with further study, or research and development work in a related area;

2. adding to your scientific knowledge with a related professional or occupation-specific qualification or gaining work experience in an area where a science background is required;

3. using your degree and the other skills you have acquired in higher education to train in a completely different field.

There are several important things to be aware of at this point.

⤵ About half of all job openings for graduates are for people from any discipline - humanities, science, social science, etc. With a science degree you could apply for many of these, plus some of the wide range of jobs requiring specialists.

⊃   After you graduate, your first job won't likely be the only job you have for the rest of your life. So if you're bored or unhappy with it, don't worry; you can always move on. Even if you think you have made the right choice, virtually everyone changes jobs as their career progresses.

⊃   You can move from more scientific into less scientific areas much more easily than the other way around.

⊃   Becoming too specialized means possible risks as well as rewards. It might lead to a dead end, or it could be the pot of gold at the end of the rainbow.

⊃   In addition to your scientific knowledge, your undergraduate studies provide opportunities to develop skills that are transferable to any working situation. These skills carry great weight with employers.

Transferable Skills: What You Can Offer Employers

Science graduates have more to offer employers than just specific scientific knowledge and skills. Employers also want the transferable skills (sometimes called "employability skills") that students learn and develop during their training. These skills and attitudes are essential for any work (paid or unpaid) you do. Transferable skills such as the following should be carefully developed.

Common Examples of Transferable (Employability) Skills

Skills	Attitudes
adaptability skills	dependability
analytical skills	integrity/honesty
problem-solving skills	concern for quality
decision-making skills	independence/initiative
communication skills	commitment to an
time-management skills	employer/work

negotiation skills   risk-taking
stress management skills   courtesy
money management skills
relationship building skills
information skills

You learn and develop these skills and attitudes in many ways all your life. Take, for example, something as seemingly simple as delivering newspapers. If you've ever had a paper route, you acquired transferable skills such as time and money management, dependability, courtesy, and independence. Even experience in the classroom, in secondary school and beyond, is a rich source of transferable skills — for example, time management, stress management, information skills, negotiation and teamwork skills, decision-making and problem-solving skills, honesty, integrity, and commitment.

As a science graduate, your studies also will have enhanced these skills in ways specifically related to sciences and technology. For example, your analytical and problem-solving skills will have been developed through laboratory and research work. Since many experiments don't work the first time, you will have learned to ask pertinent questions, interpret data critically, and deal with many variables simultaneously. You also will have learned to communicate in ways necessary to the scientific community. Skills such as recognizing what you require and knowing how to find and utilize the information are essential in today's work place.

In fact, the importance of transferable skills has been emphasized by the Conference Board of Canada, an umbrella organization whose member companies include some of the most prominent businesses (and therefore employers) in the country. The Conference Board has identified specific skills and attitudes that all employers desire, as well as a companion set of skills and attitudes (competencies) specific to work in the fields of science, technology, and mathematics. (See Appendix 2.)

If you keep these types of examples in mind, you will learn to think of yourself as possessing a collection of valuable skills and knowledge, any combination of which may be useful to a particular employer in a particular situation, rather than thinking of yourself as a "mechanical engineer" or "computer scientist," who can only fill positions with that specific label.

In Conclusion

The dividing line between jobs for scientific specialists and more general positions is not absolutely clear-cut. It's possible to move from one to the other. But the decision made at the end of a degree program as to whether or not to go further with science is critical. Remember, it is a lot easier to become less scientific in course and job progression than it is to become more so.

Many people with science degrees progress into other areas after graduating or later on in their careers. In fact, several of the young scientists profiled in this book have changed their areas of interest. Many of the skills developed while doing a science degree are transferable into other areas of work. More and more employers are recognizing this and science graduates now realize that they must possess these transferable skills if they are to compete successfully in today's world of work. Your skills and knowledge provide security in the changing workplace.

One thing is certain: there will be changes ahead. There will be changes both in the way science graduates are used by employers and in what graduates themselves want from their careers. The development of information technology, the structure of Canadian and international companies, and the growing recognition of the importance of a strong science base to the future of a successful Canadian economy will all play a part. (Career development for science graduates will be discussed in more detail in Chapter 7.)

FOUR

This chapter covers:

⊃ The context in which science graduates move on from university

⊃ The first destinations of graduates from degree programs in math, physics, chemistry, biological sciences, and combined sciences

⊃ Examples of first jobs taken by science graduates

⊃ Ways in which you can use this information.

The Background

"GRADUATE UNEMPLOYMENT RISES" is a newspaper headline people see quite often. What message does this give to someone thinking of doing a science degree?

"FOUR GRADUATES IN TEN GET JOBS" is another typical headline. This seems to imply that 60 percent of graduates are unemployed. What it *doesn't* say is how many graduates go on to postgraduate study, teaching and other professional training, take temporary jobs, or are overseas students returning home.

All universities and colleges offering degree programs have career services to help students with their career choices and with finding jobs or further courses. It is these services that collect data on what students are doing six months or more after graduation. This information can attract the attention of the media, particularly in poor economic times. When reported in the papers, the headline usually quotes graduate unemployment figures without explaining that the statistics only refer to those who have just left their programs, rather than all graduates.

The first employment figures *don't* tell you:

- ⊃ what the employment situation is like for all graduates;

- ⊃ where new graduates go after this information is collected;

- ⊃ what the equivalent unemployment rates are for those without a degree;

- ⊃ what happens to those who go on to further study or training;

- ⊃ the number of graduates taking time off to travel or do volunteer work overseas.

So Is It Worth Doing a Degree?

Completing a science degree is hard work, and university is a substantial investment of time and money. You or your family may have to make sacrifices to support your higher education and there is an expectation that this should "pay off." Many people feel that the knowledge gained in a degree program should be of immediate use and that being a graduate will give you instant status and enhanced opportunities.

There is a growing recognition of the need for a well-educated workforce if Canadians are to keep up with our industrial competitors at home and abroad. A degree is a *starting point* for many rewarding and satisfying work roles, but your ultimate success will depend more on your personal qualities than on the certificate you receive at the graduation ceremony.

Your personal qualities — values, interests, and attitudes — play an important role in your career. They influence all your decisions, so it is a good idea to understand them. For example, if you have concerns about the environment, you may be attracted to a career where you feel you can make a difference; as a result, you may choose to study areas such as alternative energy resources, sustainable agricultural practices, or wildlife preservation. Or you may have been passionate about astronomy ever since you were old enough to know what telescope was; your associated values and interests will also influence the type of work you want to do. Some people try to find employment opportunities which give them the opportunity to travel or take on short-term contracts and travel in between. If family is very important to you, you may want a work role that allows for flexible working hours. (See Chapter 7 for more on these work alternatives.)

Remember the transferable skills discussed in Chapter 3? Attitudes such as integrity, independence, initiative, and commitment are also vital in the world of work. These are also qualities that your experiences at university will have enhanced. Pursuing a degree requires commitment; getting your assignments and papers done requires initiative.

It is important to take some time to think about what really matters to you. Understanding your personal qualities will help you to make decisions working toward a satisfying career path.

A lot can happen in three or four years, so there is much to be said for selecting a degree subject about which you have enthusiasm. Selecting a subject because of the supposed employability of its graduates can be a gamble.

University careers advisor

Why Do Employers Choose Graduates?

⊃ Graduates are usually employed for their future potential and for the knowledge or experience they bring to the position. Employers expect graduates to have developed transferable skills during their time at university and in any work roles they may have held.

⊃   Graduates are expected to be "self-starters" who can manage their own work. This means they are more independent in their positions and are able to put their own personal stamp on the job.

⊃   As the working environment becomes more complicated — with new technology and legal requirements, novel industries, changing business practices, more complex products, wider markets, rising standards of living, *etc.* — so jobs become increasingly involved. As a result, employers require, and look for, well-trained and highly educated people to cope with them.

Diane Cull

This profile tells the story of a science graduate who has strived to establish herself in her chosen field of environmental conservation.

Career Profile

Age: 29
Park Ranger
High School: biology, chemistry, math
Degree: biological sciences

Diane always hoped she'd be able to find work that allowed her to pursue her two main interests: marine biology and conservation. But she was under no illusion that getting a job would be easy. At the end of her degree she scanned all the want ads. Prospective employers all wanted people who were either older or more experienced — and to make things worse, she didn't have a driver's licence.

Eventually, she found a job as a field worker on a small, local conservation project. Diane was employed on a government training scheme at minimum wage, and only for six months. But it was all practical work which came in handy later on. As a bonus, she learned to drive, too.

Then came a long hard winter of unemployment before she landed her first job in marine biology at a marine wildlife reserve. This was only three days a week, but was funded for a whole year. It was mainly educational work, talking to visitors and arranging displays. Then she had a short spell as a summer warden, another winter unemployed, followed by a short seasonal ranger job in a provincial park. This led to a research project looking at the effects of bait digging on the migrant bird population.

Eight years after leaving university, Diane finally found steady employment, as a park ranger. Her résumé lists all the courses she has attended, ranging from chain saw operation, car maintenance, and first-aid to desk-top publishing and courses on the identification of birds, trees, and marine life. All of these skills are extremely useful in the many aspects of her present post.

Diane's responsibilities as a ranger cover the upkeep of some of the park, the establishment of a nature reserve, and monitoring of the coast for wildlife, tourism, and countryside management. This makes for a varied job and one in which the organization and management of her time is entirely up to her. One day she might be supervising volunteers rebuilding bridges, the next counting wild duck on a stretch of shoreline, negotiating with a farmer about wildlife grazing, or planning a field trip with a local school.

She has regular contact with other conservation organizations, reports to a senior ranger in a town 150 km away, and has occasional contact with the rangers in other areas of the region.

Conservation jobs, if you can get one, are not highly paid, but Diane feels that the lifestyle more than compensates. "I work where other people take their holidays!" she says, smiling.

For people who want to get into this line of work, she says that the only way is by "serving an apprenticeship" as she did, through volunteer and short-term jobs, building up contacts. "That way you can develop skills in a wide range of activities: practical skills, teaching and research, wildlife identification, public relations, and people management."

Diane's enthusiasm is infectious and she feels fairly optimistic about the future for the environment. She finds that many young people are very concerned and extremely careful about their environment and even try to influence their parents' behaviour. As to her own future, she feels that she is lucky to have a job that suits her so well. Promotion to senior ranger would be a logical career move, but she is not in any hurry: "That would mean more time in the office!"

How Do New Graduates Find Jobs?

The traditional route for people leaving university was to job hunt in the final year when employers visited the universities for career fairs and recruiters travelled the country demonstrating their business and interviewing candidates on the spot. Students would apply to large companies, through their graduate recruitment schemes, for traineeships. They then make their way up through an organization by performing well in each job. Employers now recruit graduates in many different ways. The graduate traineeship route has declined in importance and involves only a small proportion of new graduates today. Most graduates now apply for specific jobs or take temporary work. This is very different from the situation when your parents' generation left university. Many graduates will have worked part- or full-time during their life at university, acquiring skills and experience that are useful to employers.

First Destinations

Not all graduates look for work immediately after finishing their programs. Many go on to graduate degrees or take training programs for specific jobs such as teaching. Others may not know what they want to do. They may want to take stock of things — do volunteer work, find short-term jobs, or spend a few months travelling. Many of these people will be counted as unemployed in the statistics collected by the universities after six months, but a year or so later they could well be on training programs or in permanent jobs. Today there are so many routes from higher education into work that the first destination figures collected by university career services only give part of the picture.

How Are Science Graduates Employed?

The following chart shows employment categories and some examples of first jobs from a sample of 100 new graduates with undergraduate degrees in science subjects. (You can find information about the destinations of those with graduate degrees in Chapter 7.) Note that the graduates' degrees weren't necessarily "prerequisites" for the jobs they found. The purpose of these data is to give you an eye-opening idea of the wide range of work that graduates can find. Your skills and knowledge can lead you into an enormous variety of career paths if you keep your thinking, and expectations, flexible.

First Jobs Found by New Graduates with Undergraduate Science Degrees

Employment Categories	Math Degree	Physics Degree	Chemistry Degree
Administration and operational management	Management trainee Administrative officer, Official Receivers Chef	Examinations assistant, Institute of Legal Executives Administrative officer, Civil Service	Management trainee Production manager, scientific publisher University administrator
Research, design and development	Design engineer	Scientific officer Research physicist Reactor physicist, nuclear industry Meteorologist Engineer	Research assistant Scientific officer R & D chemist
Scientific and engineering support services	Audio engineer	Operations trainee, water authority Trainee medical physicist Technical consultant	Medical laboratory scientific officer Laboratory technician, industrial, hospital, water authority laboratories Quality assurance officer
Environmental planning and construction			Assistant pollution control officer

Employment Categories	Math Degree	Physics Degree	Chemistry Degree
Sales, marketing and buying	Retail management trainee Customer services assistant Account executive, advertising agency	Market research trainee Marketing trainee, life assurance, food industry	Retail management trainee Sales consultant Market research trainee
Management services, computing	Management services trainee Assistant analyst, industry and public services Management consultant	Management services trainee Management consultant Computer programmer Operational research analyst Systems analyst	
Financial work	Trainee chartered accountant Management accounting trainee Insurance trainee Trainee actuary Statistician Banking trainee Investment trainee Trainee underwriter Futures market dealer	Trainee actuary Forensic accountant	Banking trainee
Legal work		Assistant, Citizens Advice Bureau	Trainee patent agent
Literary, entertainment and other creative work	Technical author, computer manufacturer Assistant theatre manager	Musician Math editor	Production editor
Information, library and museum work		Museum display technician	Library assistant, university library
Personnel work			
Health and social welfare		Community recreation coordinator	Residential social worker Milk inspector
Teaching and lecturing	Elementary teacher		
Other work	Pilot officer	Pilot officer	

Employment Categories	Computer Sciences Degree	Biological Sciences Degree	Combined Sciences Degree
Administration and operational management	Management trainee		Photofinishing store manager
Research, design and development	Research analyst	Research assistant Scientific officer	Flavour technologist Food researcher
Scientific and engineering support services	Biomechanics researcher Aerologist	Clinical trials assistant, pharmaceutical companies Field trials officer, agricultural research Laboratory technician, industrial, hospital, water authority laboratories Medical laboratory scientific officer Quality assurance officer	
Environmental planning and construction		Environmental horticulturist Pollution control officer, local government	
Sales, marketing and buying		Market research trainee Medical sales representative, pharmaceutical company	Fitness club marketing coordinator
Management services, computing	Assistant analyst, industry and public services Management services trainee Computer programmer Operational research analyst Software engineer Computer consultant Systems analyst Software designer/developer		Software engineer
Financial work		Revenue assistant, Civil Service	
Legal work			
Literary, entertainment and other creative work	Multimedia designer Assistant film editor	Assistant television producer Scientific illustrator	

Employment Categories	Computer Sciences Degree	Biological Sciences Degree	Combined Sciences Degree
Information, library and museum work		Information officer	Interpretive naturalist
Personnel work		Trainee personnel officer	
Health and social welfare		Health education officer Occupational therapist	Sports nutritionist
Teaching and lecturing		Fitness instructor	
Other work	Interior designer	Groom	Wilderness outfitter

What Does All This Mean to You?

Use your school career library and publications listed in the Resource List (page 115) to help you find out more about the occupations listed in the above chart, or any others that interest you. Remember, don't be afraid to ask people for information. You'll be surprised to discover the variety of occupations held by people you know, and they will be one of the best sources of occupational information you can find.

A science degree opens many doors...not just to what is obviously scientific work. It may be that with your degree in chemistry, physics, biology, or whatever area you have chosen, you decide to apply that specialty and become a "professional" scientist. Alternatively you may look further afield and use your personal talents to succeed in law, journalism, politics, social work, advertising or one of many other career areas that are open to graduates of any degree discipline. Remember, employers are looking at graduates not just for their academic abilities, but for their interpersonal skills. Science is not just about laboratories and test tubes, it is very often your ability to communicate your ideas effectively to others that will make you successful. Use all the non-academic activities that universities offer-clubs, societies, sports, etc., — to develop your particular personal skills and interests.

Andrew Whitmore, Career Consultant

FIVE

FURTHER STUDY — WHAT ARE THE OPTIONS?

This chapter covers:

- ⊃ The main options for further academic study and training

- ⊃ Examples of graduate degrees and professional programs taken by science graduates.

Why Study After a Degree?

Many science graduates go on to some kind of graduate study or training immediately after completing their degree, and even more will do so at different points throughout their career. There are several reasons why:

- ⊃ to develop further knowledge in their field;

- ⊃ to gain knowledge of a specialized field;

- ⊃ to learn about a related field or even move into a completely different area;

- ⊃ for enjoyment and personal challenge;

- ⊃ to gain additional knowledge or qualifications in order to take advantage of new opportunities.

In today's world of work, it is essential to maintain and continually develop your skill and knowledge base. Taking a formal advanced program is one way to do this.

The Types of Advanced Qualifications

There are three types of advanced qualifications:

1   Graduate degrees by research;

2   Graduate degrees by instruction;

3   Professional or occupation-specific courses leading to certificates or diplomas, or to professional qualifications such as teaching, medicine, accounting, law, and social work.

All of these qualifications can be full-time or part-time, although graduate degrees by research are usually full-time.

To follow the full-time route you will need to find a grant or a student loan or be self-financing. Part-time courses are often done while working, with some students receiving financial support from their employer.

There is a huge variety of graduate courses in Canada — some on very specialist topics. So when course titles are mentioned in this chapter it will probably be only one of a number in the same area of study. Only a selected few are mentioned to give a flavour of the range of options available. There are reference books with comprehensive lists of all the current courses which you would consult in the final year of your degree course. (See also the Resource List, page 115).

Graduate Degrees by Research

Graduate degrees by research lead to a doctorate (a Ph.D. or D.Phil, depending on what it's called by the university awarding it) or an M.Sc. (Master of Science). A Ph.D. takes a minimum of two years (usually four to five years), while an M.Sc. usually takes at least 12 months of full-time study or two to three years of part-time study.

Graduate degrees by research are usually taken in a university, research institute, or industrial laboratory that has a link with a university. Most universities require research students to take an M.Sc. first and then, if this goes well and funding is available, go on to a Ph.D. Some combine M.Sc. and Ph.D. programs into a single Ph.D. program.

Learning to Do Research

A degree by research involves an in-depth study of a very specific area. Each research student has an academic supervisor who acts as a guide and mentor. The results of the research are presented in a thesis — a detailed written discussion of your project — which must include work that is original and makes a contribution to the understanding of the field. Some universities also allow theses or dissertations to be comprised of a series of articles (usually published) on a single topic or highly related topics.

A graduate degree of this type is really a training program in research, and involves:

- searching through and understanding other written work in the area (called "the literature");

- constructing hypotheses about a topic;

- designing and performing experiments to test hypotheses;

- developing and using a range of scientific techniques and equipment;

- recording, analyzing, and interpreting data;

- presenting and discussing your findings at seminars and in a final thesis;

- co-operating with colleagues both in your laboratory and elsewhere.

Research as a graduate student is often thought of as a solitary occupation, with students working mainly alone in libraries. But this isn't true for scientific and technical research. A substantial portion of your time is based in a laboratory, interacting on a daily basis with other scientists in your own institute and maybe with scientists in labs around the world, through conferences and computer link-ups.

Nonetheless, what counts for your Ph.D. is your own laboratory work. You will need persistence and determination to learn the necessary techniques and to complete exacting and often repetitive practical work. Most first degree courses include some project work in addition to laboratory practical classes, and this experience will give you some idea of whether you would like research work. Although the chosen topic can be important in terms of further career progression, it often turns out that people who make a career of science find themselves working on very different subjects later on.

A graduate degree by research is not only training for academic research; many people with Ph.D. and M.Sc. qualifications also work in industry, teaching, administration, and other areas. Recent employment information has shown a very low rate of unemployment among people with a Ph.D.

Ten years after their doctorates or Master degrees, many senior scientists do very little laboratory-based work. They could be supervising other scientists or may have moved into other areas of work where the training and experience of research is of great benefit.

Funding Research Degrees

Research students get funding from a variety of different sources. There are scholarships and bursaries funded through government grants distributed through various research councils, through science-based trusts and foundations such as the Natural Sciences and Engineering Research Council, and through industrial sponsorship. The funding has to cover living expenses, research materials, and academic fees. Provincial governments also provide scholarships as do individual universities. Investigate all possibilities for assistance!

The amount provided for living expenses varies depending on the source, but it's usually less than you would get if you went into a job. People who get support from research foundations or employers are usually better off than those obtaining basic graduate student positions from a university such as teaching assistant or research assistant.

A research student has to regard this period as an integral part of career building. Whether or not the knowledge you gain during this time is directly applicable to work you want to do, education is *never* a waste of time. Remember the transferable skills discussed earlier — a graduate degree will add to your skill and knowledge base. If you are unsure about pursuing graduate studies full-time, you may wish to explore opportunities for part-time study while continuing to work. This can be done on a formal basis by enrolling in a specific degree program as a part-time student or informally by taking occasional courses in areas of interest.

Karen Farrant (see profile, page 59) is doing her Ph.D. with funding from an award which offered funding, fees, and living costs for three years. Karen is glad she decided to do a Ph.D., although she says it is difficult financially unless you have some kind of assistance. She also points out that, as a science graduate, she had always found it easy to get summer jobs and so did not graduate after her first degree with accumulated debts.

Graduate Degrees by Instruction

Master's courses include course work, lectures, and seminars, together with practical work and training in research methods. They usually end with a combination of final examinations and a short thesis.

Here are a few examples of M.Sc. courses that may be offered at the university you attend. (The course requirements are given in parentheses.)

- International agricultural marketing (any degree)

- Medical biotechnology (biological or chemical science degree)

- Interactive computer systems design (degree with significant computer science content)

- Control engineering (graduates of any discipline)

- Hydrogeology (science degree plus math beyond high school)

- Fisheries biology and management (biological sciences degree)

⊃   Opto-electronics and laser devices (electronics or physics degree)

⊃   Occupational safety and health (any degree)

⊃   Colour science (science or chemical engineering degree)

⊃   Environmental chemistry (chemistry degree)

⊃   Statistics (variety of different courses requiring different degree backgrounds)

⊃   Operational research (degree with high mathematics content)

The growth in scientific and technical knowledge is too extensive for so many specialist topics to be absorbed into undergraduate degree courses, making courses taught mainly to graduate students necessary to cover areas like these.

As you can see, these courses recruit from a wide variety of degree backgrounds. A particular subject at undergraduate degree level may be required, but this isn't always the case. Some M.Sc. courses also prefer people to have appropriate working experience. Master's degrees in areas like information science and clinical psychology involve periods of relevant practical experience and lead to professional qualifications.

For some science graduates, an M.Sc. is an introduction to a new area of work. For others, particularly those with a combined studies degree, it may involve a more specialist study of topics touched on in their first degrees. Some M.Sc. courses are arranged by employers in collaboration with a university as part of their graduate development program.

Whatever your reasons for considering further training, you will need to take stock of your situation and do some career planning. Finally, one very popular Master's degree program is the Master of Business Administration (M.B.A.). This is taken by many scientists, even those with Ph.D.s, because they want to enhance their opportunities in management. People are strongly advised to gain some working experience before embarking on an M.B.A. course. Most science graduates taking an M.B.A. are several years beyond graduation and will have managed other scientists or research teams.

Professional Degree in Education

Another popular postgraduate course is the Bachelor of Education after an approved degree, which is a requirement for graduates wishing to teach in primary or secondary schools. There is a great need for able and enthusiastic science teachers. At the secondary level there is a shortage of science teachers who are science graduates, in particular those with a physics or math degree. In many elementary schools, science graduates have an important role supporting colleagues in the teaching of science and co-ordinating the science curriculum. Look also for opportunities in training and adult education. More and more opportunities in these areas are becoming available as our population "ages."

Funding for M.Sc. and Other Taught Courses

It is, unfortunately, a lot easier to find an interesting course than it is to obtain funding to do it. As with a Ph.D. application, good grades during your undergraduate degree are essential in the competitive funding situation. Some grants are available for M.Sc. courses from the same bodies which support Ph.D. students, although an increasing number of students on full-time M.Sc. courses pay their own way either with the help of their families or student loans. Part-timers are either self-funded from earnings or supported by their employers.

Bruce Mitsumi

This profile tells the story of a science graduate who went into teaching reluctantly but found that he loved the job.

Career Profile

Age: 25
Teacher of mathematics and computing, co-ordinator for Information Technology
Favourite High School Subjects: math, physics, chemistry
Degree: statistics and management science techniques; B.Ed.

Bruce chose his high school subjects because he enjoyed math and physics, although he found physics harder. Chemistry was included because he had "vague thoughts" about being a doctor.

Operational research (OR) was what had really appealed to him. He was fascinated by the idea of applying mathematical techniques to solving practical problems like how to increase the volume of traffic going through the Suez Canal. The course included pure math, applied math, computer science, and numerical analysis. There was a choice of subjects in the second and third years. Bruce chose and computing.

In his final year Bruce had an interview with a large partnership of accountants and management consultants. This was the most popular career choice among people from his course but he says it just didn't appeal to him.

Instead, he decided to investigate teaching, although he had been determined to resist the idea up to then. ("Teaching runs in my family, and my dad's a principal.") He volunteered back at his old school and found that he loved it. He applied to university for a B.Ed. to teach mathematics.

He found the course interesting, and especially enjoyed the period of teaching practice. That confirmed his choice — teaching was it.

Bruce teaches math and information technology (IT) at the same school where he got his first job. His background in computers made him the logical choice for being "the person to call when there is anything wrong with the computer systems." He has also run workshops on IT for staff in mixed subject groups.

In addition to his teaching and technical support duties, Bruce also takes a tutor period, covering everything from extra help and study skills to relationships and sex education. Then, there are after-school responsibilities: "I coach the football team, staff meetings are every Thursday, and I attend the math and technology curriculum meeting every two weeks. And then," he jokes, "I also have a life!"

Bruce feels that teaching is the right career for him. "It's hard work but I love it," he says, before glancing at his watch and dashing off to his next class.

Professional Programs

Examples of postgraduate courses leading to a professional qualification are accounting, legal studies, personnel administration, social work, and education. Science graduates find their way into all of these fields of work.

Some courses cover similar ground to an M.Sc. but don't require training in research methods and completion of a thesis. These courses last at least nine months full-time or two years if part-time. As for other M.Sc. courses, many people doing part-time degrees are supported by their employer.

The lists below give an impression of the range of courses taken by science graduates.

Graduates in math:

Computer science
Computer systems
Education (teacher training)
Housing studies
Hydraulic engineering
Information systems
Operational research
Social administration
Statistics

Graduates in physics:

Accounting
Acoustics and noise pollution
Applied optics
Education (teacher training)
Geophysics
Information technology
Law
Materials engineering
Mathematics
Medical physics
Operational research
Process safety
Radiation and environmental protection
Semi-conductor physics
Teaching English as a Foreign Language

Graduates in chemistry:

Administration
Analytical sciences
Computing
Education (teacher training)
Information science
Law
Management studies
Marketing
Medicinal chemistry

Graduates in biological sciences:

Biotechnology
Ecotoxicology
Education (teacher training)
Ergonomics
Export management
Genetic counselling
Immunology

Information technology
Journalism
Marine resource development
Nutrition
Printing and publishing
 technology
Scientific illustration

What Next After a Graduate Degree?

The career services offices in universities and colleges are not only used by undergraduates; if you are in a postgraduate program or are studying for a graduate degree, you'll need advice too. Most science departments have contacts with industry and with other university departments in North America and overseas. When you decide what you want to do they can help you to make contacts, particularly if you are in a specialist program. Most departments should also be able to provide information about the jobs taken up by students who have recently completed their postgraduate program.

Academic Research

If you want to continue in academic research after completing a Ph.D., you can go on to a postdoctoral fellowship either in Canada, the United States, or overseas. These fellowships are seen as a way of broadening your research experience and giving you time to find more permanent employment. Canadian scientists are encouraged to do this, and many do — mainly to the United States and Europe. A small percentage of people with science Ph.D.s do postdoctoral work. If your goal is to teach at a university, you'll almost certainly need to do postdoctoral research in order to obtain a position.

Opportunities to work in a research setting overseas are predominantly in the sciences. Funding for postdoctoral fellowships, including travel and other expenses, is available from a variety of sources: university departments, research councils, charities, and international organizations such as NATO.

Research Difficulties

Work opportunities for research scientists are affected by the way research is funded. There are now more collaborative projects between science research departments and industry, and more scientists are moving into industry at later stages of their careers.

The trend in research funding in recent times has been toward short-term grants from government and other bodies, with staff working on temporary contracts. As a result, the time taken for young researchers to progress to a permanent post has lengthened.

Research science can also put a great strain on young families. Because career advancement and future funding depend on the researcher's early success at a postdoctoral level, long and irregular hours in the laboratory are the norm for those who want to succeed.

First Employment Information

First employment information about those with graduate degrees is published every year by many individual universities and colleges. When funds permit it, a university's career service will survey recent graduates (usually six months after graduation) to find out if they are employed and if the job held is related to the graduate's field of study. Some surveys also include starting salary information. The results of the survey are usually available to the public through the university's career service and through the yearly *Maclean's Guide to Canadian Universities*. High school libraries or guidance/career counsellors may also keep copies of universities' and colleges' graduate placement surveys.

Points to Note About First Destinations of Those with Graduate Degrees

⊃ There are more students with graduate degrees than ever before.

⊃ Those with graduate degrees are more likely to find jobs than those with undergraduate degrees.

⊃   Many people with an M.Sc. go on to do a Ph.D.

Points to Note About First Employment of Those with Graduate Degrees

⊃   Students who complete a graduate degree are much more likely to go into jobs in research, design, and development related to their degree subject.

⊃   A large percentage of those with graduate degrees in mathematics and computer science go into computer careers.

⊃   A small proportion of people with graduate degrees in science go into financial careers.

Making a Choice

The science graduates in the profiles who did graduate studies and professional programs had many different reasons for doing so. Janine Pelletier (page 26) is doing an M.Sc. organized by her employer at her place of work, whereas Aaron Devoretsky (page 29) is studying for professional exams part-time. Karen Farrant (page 59) needed a Ph.D. to become a research scientist, while Bruce Mitsumi (page 51) took a B.Ed. to become a teacher.

If you are interested in obtaining a graduate degree or completing another professional program, you should start applying very early in the final year of your undergraduate course. Information about opportunities is available through the career services office in universities and through university departments. If you're already employed or are applying for jobs, you should also discuss the options with your (prospective) employer.

To Summarize

⊃   In all, upwards of half of all graduates in physics, chemistry, and biology are likely to do a graduate degree or diploma immediately after their first degree.

People with honours degrees are even more likely to go on to further study.

⊃ Computer science and engineering graduates are most likely to go straight into work.

⊃ A small percentage of all science graduates go into teacher training. The employment prospects in teaching for science graduates are considered good, especially if you're prepared to teach in smaller communities.

⊃ Graduate degrees may involve both instruction and research. Most diploma courses are taught courses and often have practical experience built in.

⊃ Ph.D.s are trained in research, although only a small proportion of Ph.D. graduates go into academic research. Those who do usually take a postdoctoral fellowship as the next stage.

⊃ Most employers pay a higher starting salary to new employees with graduate degrees, although the amount varies considerably.

SIX

INTERNATIONAL OPPORTUNITIES

This chapter covers:

⊃ The international nature of science

⊃ Studying and working abroad at different stages.

Scientists Abroad

The international nature of science means there are many opportunities for science graduates to work or study overseas at some stage of their careers. Multinational organizations, world trade, and commerce all offer the chance to travel and work abroad.

At present, many young scientists in academic research are finding it difficult to get more than short-term contracts, so they are looking abroad. In the United States and Europe, young scientists may find more job security, higher salaries, and better funding for equipment. At the same time, many young scientists from other countries are coming to Canada for postgraduate and postdoctoral training before returning home. People also seek work abroad at a later stage in their careers because they may feel that opportunities are limited in Canada.

There are a variety of ways you can make the international nature of science work for you.

- By taking all or part of an undergraduate course abroad
- By taking a postgraduate course abroad
- By taking a postdoctoral training abroad
- By finding a permanent job in another country
- By finding a job that takes you abroad
- By working for a multinational company
- Through government and international organizations
- Through casual work and volunteer projects.

All or Part of an Undergraduate Program Abroad

Studying for a first degree at a university outside of Canada, and particularly overseas, is not a very practical idea for most people. There are numerous difficulties to overcome: education systems in other countries may be very different, courses can be much longer, and it is unlikely grants will be available — you would have to take care of your living expenses as well as the tuition fees. (You also need to be fluent in the relevant language, although this isn't much of a problem in English-speaking countries!)

It's much more feasible to choose a degree that allows you to spend time in a university abroad as part of your undergraduate program. There are various schemes that will enable you to do this. Many universities have exchange programs with universities in the United States, Great Britain, or continental Europe. These are popular courses and get a lot of applicants.

Karen Farrant

After spending a year studying in France as part of her undergraduate course, the science graduate in this profile is now working on a research project in collaboration with a French university.

Career Profile

Age: 24
Research Student
Favourite High School Subjects: mathematics, chemistry
Degree: chemistry with additional studies in French

When Karen started high school she wanted to keep her options open by combining science and languages. She had no idea about what she wanted to do at this stage so she chose the subjects she enjoyed with the knowledge that math with chemistry still left open a wide range of science-related careers if she chose to go that way.

Karen enjoyed chemistry in high school and chose her degree course carefully, although she was warned by summer job employers to avoid being "neither one thing nor another." She was attracted to her degree course because it offered a full chemistry major with some French studies, with the extra attraction of spending a year at the Grande École in Lyon, France.

The part of the course in Canada was hard work because the French language was over and above a full chemistry degree course program. In the language classes the emphasis was on spoken French with lessons in technical French. It helped enormously with her confidence during her time in Lyon.

The Grande École was seen as a very elite institution, although it was much larger than the university at home. Karen attended huge whole class tutorials and found that the French students were much less experienced in laboratory work. At home, male students outnumbered the women by about two to one, and all the professors were male. In Lyon the student population was 50:50 and there were female role-models on the academic staff.

Although none of the academic results on the French part of her course counted toward her degree, Karen wanted a qualification to demonstrate her proficiency, having worked so hard on her French. So she took the Institute of Linguists final examinations — a degree-level qualification.

Karen felt that she and her fellow students who went to France really grew up during the year. "Having coped with the totally different environment, language, and culture, we were really better equipped to cope with life after university."

Back in Canada, Karen chose a final year option in medical chemistry because of her interest in the drug industry. She was advised during a summer job with a pharmaceutical company that she should at least get a Ph.D. Her professor gave her some names of centres where this sort of work was going on and she sent around her résumé. She was very lucky to be just in time to be considered for an award which offered funding, fees, and living costs for three years for a research project on AIDS in collaboration with Montpellier University in France. She was an ideal candidate and won the fellowship.

She is now working on a project trying to inhibit the enzyme which is involved in coating the HIV virus before it leaves one infected cell to infect another. She is collaborating with French scientists and working for part of the time in France. She finds that science and scientists have a higher prestige in Europe, and she enjoys the greater equality that women have in French science.

Karen says her Ph.D. is going well, but she is not yet sure if she wants to stay in research after finishing. The international aspects of patent work still appeal to her, but she is also keen to work in the drug industry. Whichever way she goes, Karen seems to be in a very strong position, with excellent science qualifications, language skills, and experience.

Finding a Program

There are a number of undergraduate programs that will give you the chance to study languages as well as science. These could be combined programs in science and languages, but more often they are programs like the one Karen Farrant did — with language study alongside a full science degree. Languages in high school are not always required in order to do this kind of course, although clearly they would be a help.

Some students in applied science courses are lucky enough to be offered work experience abroad in their co-op year. Again, language skills come in very handy. Taking time out of your university program for a work placement is common practice in many countries. It's a way for employers to try out potential employees with no long-term commitment. Such placements can be obtained through university departments or through exchange programs.

Every year there are new programs, and the details of the existing ones may change. You can also find out more from some of the materials in the Resource List, from university departments, and from university career services offices. There is now much more information available through all career services offices about studying and working abroad.

A Postgraduate Program Abroad

Some opportunities are available through UNESCO, which produces a book on study overseas giving details of funding arrangements. At present, scientists make up about a quarter of postgraduates taking UNESCO fellowships, with France and Germany being the countries taking most. Some people choose to study overseas after gaining some working experience at home first.

Every year a number of young science graduates go to the United States to do graduate training leading towards a doctorate. The funding comes through each university department; in the private universities like Stanford and Yale, no particular preference is given to American students. There are other sources of funding such as scholarships from the Fulbright Commission. A Canadian student with a very strong academic record has a good chance of being accepted.

Postdoctoral Training Abroad

The most common way for young research scientists to get experience abroad is at postdoctoral level. Short-term placements called "post doctorates," usually lasting two to three years, are an excellent opportunity to broaden your experience and establish contacts in American and European universities and research institutes. Grants and travel scholarships are provided by funding bodies such as NSERC (National Science and Engineering and Research Council) and NATO. Competition is fierce, with applicants from all over the world, but many young scientists with PhDs take up "postdocs" abroad every year.

If you want to take advantage of the international nature of research science, this is the route for you. It is an opportunity that is unique to science postgraduates; it is almost unknown in other academic subjects.

In scientific research especially there are opportunities in "intra-national" collaborative research laboratories, as well as in universities and research institutions. Prestigious institutes will compete to attract the best scientists no matter what their nationality, and they will usually recruit people with a proven track record in their own country. Specialist skills can be a great advantage and scientists working in rapidly expanding areas of research, such as gene cloning or super-conductivity, may suddenly find themselves very employable in other countries.

A Permanent Job in Another Country

Is it really possible for new science graduates to get their first jobs in other countries?

It happens, but it's very unusual — only a small percentage get permanent jobs abroad immediately following graduation. Many more new graduates take temporary jobs, and of those finding permanent jobs abroad, most do so after they have first gained experience from a Canadian base. At the postgraduate level, the proportion working abroad straight away is higher, not including those doing postdoctoral fellowships.

There are a number of reasons why so few graduates get their first jobs abroad.

The difficulties:

- Higher education systems differ.

- Weak language skills or a lack of understanding of different cultures can also cause problems.

- Each country has graduates of its own and may well prefer to employ them. Employers may need to get a work permit for an employee who is not a citizen. This could prove difficult if there are suitable locals who could do the job.

⊃   A new graduate is less likely to have much useful experience to offer. Employers in the United States and most European countries prefer to employ graduates with "relevant" degrees; there are fewer jobs for which any degree would be acceptable.

In spite of these difficulties, if you are determined and well prepared you may still succeed; there are always exceptions.

Possible solutions:

⊃   Improve your language skills. A knowledge of other languages is a great asset if you want to live and work abroad.

⊃   If you have a graduate degree you are more likely to succeed.

⊃   If you want to work abroad and do not have higher qualifications or contacts, it will help to get some job experience first so you have more to offer an employer.

⊃   Links with companies through an exchange scheme, or through temporary work, will give you an advantage.

⊃   Another strategy is to join a Canadian company that might offer the chance to work abroad later on, or to apply to a multinational company with branches all over the world. (See below.)

Where Are the Jobs?

Some European countries have shortages of trained scientists, as well as engineers and computer scientists. However, the opening up of Eastern Europe has altered the dynamics of the labour market in Europe and scientists from the East are now competing for jobs and training in the West.

There are opportunities for experienced staff in many African countries in agriculture, engineering, science teaching, and other areas. There is some direct recruitment but this is mainly through organizations like CIDA and CUSO.

Middle-eastern countries — particularly the major oil-producing countries who are undergoing economic expansion — advertise for staff in the newspapers. They usually require senior managers and qualified professionals who have experience related to the petrochemical or construction industries. Although attractive (tax-free) salaries are offered, it is important to consider carefully the implications of living and working in a country with a very different culture.

In Australia and the United Kingdom there may be less of a cultural difference, but there are fewer opportunities. Because of the difficulties involved in obtaining work permits, only those foreigners with very specialized qualifications and experience have a chance, especially during an economic recession. A Canadian-owned company in Australia would find the same obstacles to hiring a Canadian scientist as a U.S.-owned company would when trying to employ an American citizen in Malaysia.

In Japan and other "Pacific rim" countries like Taiwan and Malaysia, the rapid growth of high-tech industries may well lead to increased opportunities for science graduates in the future.

A Job that Takes You Abroad

Canada has commercial and cultural interests throughout the world. As a result, some Canadian companies require their staff to work abroad for varying periods. Although improved communications mean fewer staff are now sent to live abroad permanently, an increasing number are going out for shorter periods from a Canadian base.

As Canadian firms begin to see themselves as more and more international in their business action, they may find it worthwhile to establish bases in other countries, with staff moving back and forth. Many Canadian companies are now keen to provide young workers with experience abroad early in their careers.

Janine Pelletier (page 26) is in constant contact with people working on telecommunications research and development, particularly in Japan and the United States where scientists are at the forefront of her particular area of work. She has to keep up-to-date with worldwide developments in her field in order to advise her company about them.

Aaron Devoretsky (page 29) visits the European Patent Office in The Hague or Munich and the U.S. Patent Office in Washington. Chandra Persaud's job with Shell (page 67) has taken him to Oman for three years.

Marketing and technical staff in particular are now more likely to be based in Canada and sent abroad on a regular basis. There are also increasing numbers of consultancies, in finance and computing for example, and more recently in industries such as transportation, water treatment, mining, and especially telecommunications. These firms are competing for work around the world, often working for government departments. Their staff are required to travel extensively, working on short-term projects in different countries.

Business travel is usually highly structured and designed to fit in the maximum amount of work in the minimum time away from the home base. Your evenings may also be taken up with work-related activities and your weekends spent on planes, either moving on to the next destination or flying back home to start again on Monday morning. Travelling for work is far from a vacation: there are few opportunities to go sightseeing on a business trip. Scientists who travel to academic conferences, however, often find that the pace is more relaxed and can be combined with a few days of leisure.

Working for a Multinational Company

Many young graduates apply to join a multinational company in the hope that they will have the chance to travel and work abroad. The idea of working for a multinational may sound glamorous, but staff do not always have a great deal of choice about where they work or how much time they will spend outside Canada. The opportunity to travel depends on the nature of the business and the way the firm organizes staff development and promotion. Language skills are always a great asset, no matter which country you visit, and can help you overcome some of the cultural differences that prevent many visitors from integrating into the local community. Language and cultural barriers often mean that social life is restricted to the company or an expatriate community within the "host" country.

Chandra Persaud

The chemistry graduate in this profile was sent by his company to work in Oman, in the Persian Gulf.

Career Profile

Age: 28
Head of Network Development
Shell Marketing (OMAN) Ltd.
Favourite High School Subjects: physics, chemistry, math
Degree: chemistry

Chemistry was always Chandra's best subject, and his degree program appealed to him because the four-year course included a year of research. He considered going into research, but after a summer job in a lab he decided this wasn't the career he wanted. He was attracted to marketing instead. He says, "Marketing had a sort of glamour. Everyone has views on marketing." He applied to Shell as a graduate trainee and was accepted.

Chandra's first job involved deciding what goods should be put in gas station shops. After that he spent a year as a business analyst, which provided an environment for developing his computer skills. Four years later, he was sent to Oman in the Persian Gulf to oversee the running of the country's 113 gas stations. On arrival, Chandra was sent on a one-week course explaining how to behave respectfully in the country. For his career, he says this was a super job. He describes Oman as "a beautiful country isolated by ocean, mountains, and desert, with a wonderful climate."

Chandra is now head of network development for gas stations across the whole of Oman. This involves planning the building of new gas stations and opening extra shops. He helps the developers with buying the land, planning and building the premises, and running the business. Negotiations are carried out in English but he has picked up some Arabic along the way.

Chandra enjoys working in such a different culture. He finds the Omani people "very charming to work with. And it is important to understand the differences in order to do business," he says. For instance, one of the Shell oils is yellow, a colour that the Omanis associate with illness and bad luck. Chandra says that green is a much more suitable colour and would sell better!

Chandra has found the quality of training at Shell to be very high. He has had a series of jobs but has also been given on-going training and helpful assessment. Shell puts a strong emphasis on using experience and identifying transferable skills. Although it has been unobtrusive, he feels that his career development is being carefully planned and monitored.

Chandra has found his chemistry background a great help, but he says any technical background would have been appropriate, particularly one which included math and computing. "If you work in an industry like this you are surrounded by technology, and you must be able to understand the product as well as computer programs, information management, and production processes."

Government and International Organizations

A number of government departments have opportunities for people who wish to travel and work for periods overseas. The Departments of External Affairs and Defense are obvious examples. You might also consider international organizations such as the World Bank or the United Nations and its related organizations. Not all these organizations specifically recruit scientists, but many science graduates have a lot to offer. Although there aren't many science graduates working for them at present, there should be greater opportunities in the future. More and more often, the focus of international diplomacy and international relations is on technical and scientific problems. Well-trained and articulate people will be needed to solve them.

Casual Work and Volunteer Projects

Before they decide on a particular career, many students choose to spend some time after they finish their degree courses living and working abroad. If you would like to see more of the world in this way, there is a wide range of routes you can take.

Lots of new graduates take short-term casual work, and scientists are no exception. You could experience life on a kibbutz in Israel, apply to go to the U.K. on a "working holiday" visa, work on the ski slopes of New Zealand, or help on an international work camp. The Student Work Abroad Program (SWAP), for example, will arrange required legal documentation, provide travel and working holiday information, and offers some services in the host countries for participants. Another well-known example is JET, the Japan Exchange and Teaching Program.

Voluntary organizations are usually looking for people with special skills and often ask for a longer-term commitment. In developing countries there are often opportunities for agriculture graduates, medical staff, and engineers. New math and science graduates are also sought for teaching jobs. CUSO (formerly known as Canadian University Service Overseas) is probably the best known of these groups, placing volunteer graduates in third world postings.

As a volunteer you could end up working in a remote area so you need to be pretty self-reliant, although you will be thoroughly briefed in Canada before you go. Relevant work experience is in great demand, as most projects aim to provide local people with self-sufficiency and independence through practical training.

Summary

At every level, the international nature of science offers graduates a wide range of options.

If you decide to go into a scientific job, you will be aware of scientific developments in other countries from your first degree right through your career. You will communicate with other science specialists all over the world, through computer networks, conferences, visits, study, and research projects overseas.

In scientific research there is an international community in each area of specialization, and there are always opportunities in laboratories and research institutes around the world.

Science graduates go into many other jobs with an international dimension, involving travel or working for periods abroad. For most people, these opportunities come after first gaining some experience in Canada.

This may sound as if a science degree alone is a free ticket to travel the world, but there are other factors involved. Jobs abroad often require additional skills and experience and there will be keen competition from scientists from other countries. Having said that, there are many ways in which you can enhance your chances of working abroad.

Canadian scientists have a distinct advantage in that English is the international language of science. However, although your scientific peers may understand written English and be able to conduct technical discussions, companies abroad operate mostly in the language of the country where they are based. So for many science-related jobs and other careers that take you outside Canada, language skills are a great asset.

Many science graduates work abroad for some of their working lives, and some emigrate permanently, living and bringing up their families in their new, chosen country. If the idea of an international career appeals to you, you'll need a high level of expertise in a field that is in demand, together with a working knowledge of at least one other major language and the desire to experience a new way of life.

SEVEN

YOUR FUTURE AS A SCIENCE GRADUATE

This chapter covers:

- ⊃ Work alternatives
- ⊃ Career building for science graduates
- ⊃ Future demand for science graduates.

Vital Statistics

This book has introduced you to the wide range of first jobs for science graduates, but these are just the starting points. People change work roles and develop in many different ways. For instance, more and more young graduates are taking contract or consulting positions or going on to further study. This chapter looks at work alternatives and career building for science graduates.

Information on the career progression of science graduates is difficult to track because people move around and university career service departments lose touch with them. Anecdotal evidence is not very reliable; the employment situation changes very quickly so the stories you hear now about future opportunities may be out of date when you get to that stage. Globalization, changes in corporate structures, technological developments, and political changes in Canada, the United

States, and the rest of the world are all factors that affect the supply of work and the lives of the people doing the work. The people who are in senior positions today probably started out 30 or 40 years ago. Things were very different then, and they will continue to change as you progress through your working life.

Career Building for Science Graduates

You may not have realized it, but you have been building your career for years. Each decision you make moves you closer to or further from the future you have imagined for yourself. Looked at in this way, every decision is a career decision.

Take a minute to think about that. For example, what if you decide to travel in Europe for a summer. You're probably thinking, "How can that possibly be a career decision? If anything, all it does is leave a blank spot on my résumé!" However, while you're enjoying the sights, you're also learning language skills, being independent and responsible, exploring new opportunities, negotiating and building relationships — all of which are useful skills in any career. Understanding the values, interests, and beliefs which motivate your decisions will help you move you toward your preferred future. As a science graduate, you have the added bonus of an extremely valuable knowledge base developed during your course work. Your skills and knowledge are your security in the changing world of work.

Adaptability is another essential characteristic for success. This is true for everyone — from huge corporations to self-employed individuals. Spontaneity and serendipity must also be taken into consideration. Serendipity refers to the ability to find worthwhile things without specifically seeking them. You never know when you may be presented with an interesting opportunity; so, while planning for your future is important, it's equally important to not let yourself become limited by your own planning.

Work Alternatives

The following table describes the work alternatives emerging from the changing world of work. None of the alternatives are considered better or worse — they are simply different.

They all exist in the workplace in a variety of combinations. You'll notice that they are listed in order of increasing levels of personal and financial risk. However, risk is a matter of individual comfort. What one person finds risky, another finds exciting. When you are considering work alternatives, it's important to think about your values, beliefs, and interests. For example, if security, flexibility, and variety are very important to you, job- or work-sharing may be options to consider. If you plan to pursue a formal education program, you may wish to find short-term contracts to fill in the time between semesters. Or, if you like to travel, finding longer-term consulting work which allows for breaks between projects may be the way to go.

Keep in mind that the advantages and disadvantages noted in the last two columns are a matter of perspective. A disadvantage to one person may be an advantage to another. It's up to you to decide what is advantageous and disadvantageous about each work alternative. Remember also that you will change over your career, so being aware of trends and opportunities will ensure you continue to move toward your preferred future.

An Overview of Work Alternatives

Work Alternative	Description	Advantages	Disadvantages
Full-Time Employment	Working to a job description for a single employer more than 30 hours/week	• Sense of security and stability • Predictable income • Predictable duties • Employment benefits • Feeling of permanence, of belonging	• Limited control (not your own boss) • Security may be an illusion • Limited flexibility when laid off or fired • Usually limited opportunity for financial success
Part-Time Employment	Working to a job description for a single employer less than 30 hours/week	• Sense of security and stability • Predictable income • Predictable duties • Feeling of permanence, of belonging Free time to pursue • other interests	• Less income and fewer benefits • Security may be an illusion • Limited flexibility when laid off or fired • Usually limited opportunity for financial success

Work Alternative	Description	Advantages	Disadvantages
Multi-Tracking	Working within two or more jobs at the same time	• Able to pursue a variety of interests • Increased flexibility in times of change due to a diverse skill set • Security that comes with not having all one's eggs in one basket	• Can put pressure on leisure time • Requires strong time-management skills
Job Sharing	Working with one or more people within a single job description for a single employer	• Sense of security and stability • Predictable income • Predictable duties • Employment benefits • Feeling of permanence, of belonging • Free time to pursue other interests	• Limited control (not your own boss) • Security may be an illusion • Limited flexibility when laid-off or fired • Usually limited opportunity for financial success
Work Sharing	Working with one or more people to perform a function or set of functions for a single employer	• Some security, stability • Diversity and flexibility in work • Feeling part of a team • Some independence, decision-making • Predictable income • Employment benefits	• Some unpredictability in work tasks • Often high pressure from peers to perform well • Sometimes requires extra effort and time that is unpaid
Talent Pooling	Working within a group of individuals with common interests but usually different talents. Each person markets for the others.	• Can meet many needs with the help of pool members, thus expanding the amount of work available • Because everyone markets, "work search" time is reduced • Can focus on a work specialty (do what you really want to do) • Creates the appearance of a large operation without all the costs and commitment associated with entrepreneurship; it is easier to opt out	• Fairly high unpredictability in terms of where the next work is coming from • Requires exceptional team and relationship skills • Always must be ready for pool members to move on

Work Alternative	Description	Advantages	Disadvantages
Agent/Broker	Marketing and/or representing the products and/or services of others	• Opportunity to meet many people in many settings • Opportunity to be creative • Considerable potential for financial success	• No employment benefits • Can take some time to build up a base of talent to represent • Considerable unpredictability in terms of income
Contracting	Working within a specified job description for a specific, contracted period of time for a single employer	• Opportunity to work in different settings; have variety • Can plan for long gaps between contracts for holidays • Feeling of independence; not "stuck" with a specific employer	• Usually no employment benefits • Limited security • Unpredictable income over the long term • Paper work and accounting
Consulting	Working to complete specific tasks within specific time frames on a number of projects simultaneously	• Considerable flexibility in schedule • Considerable variety in work and work settings • Potential for high income • Independence • Ability to do the work you want to do	• Constant pressure to find the next project (every day is a work search day) • Unpredictable income • Often requires long hours with little financial return • Paper work and accounting
Self-Employment	Developing, producing and marketing services and/or products in a one-person operation	• Considerable flexibility in schedule • Potential for high income • Independence • Ability to do the work you want to do	• Constant pressure to keep sales up • Unpredictable income especially at start-up • Often requires long hours with little financial return • Often requires investments that may be lost • Paper work and accounting

Work Alternative	Description	Advantages	Disadvantages
Entrepreneurship	Developing, producing and marketing services and/or products in an operation which involves managing others	• Considerable flexibility in schedule • Potential for high income • Independence • Ability to do the work you want to do	• Constant pressure to keep sales up • Unpredictable income, especially at start-up • Often requires long hours with little financial return • Often requires investments that may be lost • Constant pressure to pay staff; to not let them down • Paper work and accounting

Source: *Radical Change in the World of Work: Workbook.* Alberta Advanced Education and Career Development, 1996.

Moving from Research to Other Areas

The difficult thing for graduates working in research is to decide when the time is right to move out of research, if this is what you wish to do. It is very difficult as a new graduate to know which way your skills and interests will lead you at different stages of your career. Research in industry attracts a very different individual from the one who prefers development work — turning ideas into potential products, overseeing pilot production testing, and scaling up. Some science graduates do get more interested in development work later on in their careers, but others decide to move into quite different areas. These include:

➲ Research management

➲ Development work

➲ Project management

➲ Production management

➲ Quality assurance

➲ Marketing — market assessment

⊃ Licensing of intellectual property

⊃ Commercial development

⊃ Information technology

A crucial element of career building is avoiding the dead end — unless, of course, you are happy "there." Being able to move to other areas, using your expertise in a different setting, learning new skills, having the chance to try new roles — these are all more desirable in a career than edging up predetermined structures and waiting around for positions to open. Responsibility for your career planning is your own, so it is vital to understand both your own skills and knowledge and the opportunities emerging from the changing world of work. Doing so will put you in a position to benefit from these changes and move you closer to your preferred future.

Career Progression and Hierarchy

The structure of business operations has been changing over the past several years. For example:

⊃ Organizations are becoming "flatter" and less hierarchical, with layers of middle management removed.

⊃ There's a growing need for specialists educated to a high level, who will tend not to be managers of other staff.

⊃ There's an expectation that graduates will assume more responsible roles sooner than they would have done in the past.

⊃ Service industries and the professions are re-thinking their productivity and what they will require for both recruitment and retention of staff.

These changes are positive for many science graduates. In the future, more young families probably will have two graduate parents, both of whom may want to pursue a career. The opportunity to continue in a specialization without feeling the pressure to go for traditional career advancement and join a management hierarchy might be seen as a great advantage. The move toward less formal working relationships may help people to balance their professional roles more comfortably with their personal lives.

Where Will the Work Be?

Jobs may be scarce, but work is plentiful.

Barrie Day, Career Development Practitioner

There are several areas in which science graduates are well-positioned to find, or create, work opportunities. For example, changes to the structure of government are often viewed as negative or limiting by workers. However, these changes are also creating new opportunities. With downsizing has come a trend toward contracting out professional and technical work for set periods of time or for specific projects. Increasingly, government at all levels is looking to the private sector for joint-venture projects in research and development applications. In addition, a financial base is being established, especially by the federal government, to support grants to the private sector for technical innovation in areas such as pharmaceuticals, medical research, and environmental research. Becoming aware of trends such as these will help you anticipate the opportunities emerging from the changing structure of government.

In academic science, shortages are predicted. If young academics are not recruited now, there will be unfilled vacancies in higher education when the present generation retires. There will be a continuing demand from the schools (elementary and secondary) and from further education as the importance of science and technical education is more fully realized.

The general public's increasing interest in science and science-related issues means more opportunities for science graduates in the media and in communications. The continual growth of scientific knowledge requires explanation and interpretation; this will lead to work in areas like specialist communications, information science, technical publishing, and journalism.

Information technology (IT) will continue to dominate communications at all levels of industry, commerce, and public and private life. Again, scientist graduates are in a strong position to find opportunities here. The IT knowledge and experience gained on your degree program will be a great asset in all sorts of jobs and will give you an advantage over less IT-literate graduates at all levels.

The internationalization of science-based companies will also continue to increase opportunities in the United States, Europe, and further afield — especially in developing countries where growth depends on scientific and technical expertise. In the near future, science graduates may find themselves in increasing demand because the proportion of people studying science is not keeping pace with the need for workers with a strong scientific knowledge base.

Summary

Not all science graduates want to run large industries or stalk the corridors of power. Many want to work in some aspect of science because it interests them and they feel it is worthwhile. They feel they can make important contributions to the development of knowledge, to education, to the application of science to problems for the benefit of our own standard of living and economy, as well as to global problems such as poverty, hunger and the environment. Some science graduates see themselves as scientists all their working lives. Others use their scientific training as managers, teachers, librarians, publishers, agricultural advisors, actuaries, or patent agents.

Different roles suit different people at different stages of their careers. The work you choose early on in your career may not be the right one in a few years' time. By being adaptable, maintaining and developing your transferable skills and knowledge, understanding work alternatives, and observing trends, you can create opportunities for yourself.

Caroline Chichioco

The math graduate in this profile handles investments worth millions of dollars in her job as portfolio manager for a life assurance company.

Career Profile

Age: 29
Portfolio Manager
Favourite High School Subjects: English, history, math, physics, French
Degree: mathematics

Caroline had trouble deciding between arts and math when it came time to choose her university degree. Eventually, "I chose math because it was the subject I felt I had a natural aptitude for. But I didn't have a clue about what I wanted to do afterwards."

Caroline studied at a small university and "loved the sense of community. It had a great student life, too." As for her courses, "They were challenging, but hard work — more so than I expected. Still, they were very rewarding personally. I felt I had really accomplished something."

Still unsure about the work she wanted to do, Caroline eventually took a job doing actuarial work, which fit well with her math. Actuaries use mathematical techniques to solve financial problems and predict the financial implications of different actions. She realized pretty quickly that this choice was a mistake. "It wasn't for me. Sometimes it's not until you're actually in a job that you become aware of what would suit you. This didn't suit me. On the other hand, it did get me interested in the investment world. I just knew I wanted a much broader view of it."

So Caroline found work with a stockbroker as an investment analyst. This meant finding out about companies, their financial records, business strategies, and the competitors, then making recommendations about buying or selling shares. Her clients were investment managers in life assurance companies and fund management houses.

After this experience, Caroline moved on to the life assurance company where she now works as a portfolio manager. She is responsible for nearly one billion dollars of share holdings. Decisions are needed on which shares to buy, sell, and hold on to. There are new share offerings all the time, and companies are changing continually. Caroline has to meet the directors of companies she is considering, do further research, and then make an assessment. Information comes from all kinds of sources: computer databases, research documents, and company reports, but mostly through meetings with the company management.

"I feel I'm in a privileged position," says Caroline. "There's constant variety and a lot of contact with people. I also love the competitive edge and the pressure! And my math degree really comes in handy, because it gives me a lot of credibility. Actually, I use my math very little in the job, but it's valuable training for approaching problems in a logical and thorough manner."

EIGHT

WHERE DO YOU GO FROM HERE?

This chapter covers:

- Taking stock of where you are
- Planning your next step
- Sources of information and advice.

Your Career, Your Decision

This final chapter is about what you can do now to help yourself make decisions, make progress, and implement your plans. You will find lots of suggestions of things to do, people to talk to, and information to use. You need to investigate your own values and interests as well as assess the different opportunities that are available.

If all this sounds difficult, it is. But it's vitally important to you. You will find so much of your time gets taken up with short-term issues: assignments, exams, social activities, holidays. Your degree and career choices are important and deserve your attention. It is your future and only you can make it work.

Source of Information and Advice

Computer-based Career Information Systems

Most schools, libraries, and career centres have Internet access to interactive computer databases that provide information on careers related to your interests and subjects. A good starting point is CanWorkNet, a site set up by Human Resources Development Canada to help people with career development issues. CanWorkNet's address is http://www.canworknet.ca.

Computer-based Guidance Systems

Many schools and career centres have access to CHOICES or *Discover*, computer-based programs designed to help students identify potential career paths. You can use them to obtain information about specific occupations and post-secondary institutions/programs. These computer-based personal guidance systems have you respond to items on a questionnaire. Your responses are processed by the computer, which then gives you a personal print-out of work suggestions. This will help you to choose the subjects which leave open a good range of career paths that interest you.

There are other interactive computer-based systems available, so ask about them in your school, university, or local careers centre. For example, the CD-ROMs *Career Cruising* and *School Finder* will prove useful.

The Media

Equinox, Discover, and *Scientific American* are three of the many science magazines available at newsstands, local libraries, and many schools. They have lots of news about developments in sciences, as well as some careers articles. Reading about science and watching TV science programs such as those on the Discovery Channel, Life Network, and public broadcasting stations can also help you to identify where your scientific interests lie.

Alternative Courses

Don't forget you could do a co-op course or get work experience as part of your degree course. You might also consider a course with an American or European link or one which will give you the chance to study or work abroad.

Alternative Qualifications

Remember, there is a whole range of diploma courses, often with less stringent entry requirements than university. Some universities will give you transfer credit for some or all of the courses in a diploma program, depending on the program. This could be a good alternative to a degree course if that's what you'd prefer to do.

Work Experience and Work Shadowing

Many schools have work experience programs which give you the chance to work in an organization and find out about the jobs people do. Some students are able to find part-time or summer jobs in an area that interests them. Talk to your parents, relatives, and friends. They may be able to answer your questions about a certain industry or even help you find a summer or part-time job.

Work shadowing involves spending a day or two following someone doing a particular job, watching them at work, and seeing and hearing about the job first-hand. This is often a good way to get to know about the tasks involved in higher-level jobs which you would be less likely to be able to try out on a summer or part-time job.

Ask your careers/guidance advisor or your science teachers about these schemes. Female students who would like to meet, or shadow, female science or engineering graduates can make contact through the local branch of WISE. Ask your science teachers to help you.

Higher Education Conventions

Many career service departments run events where you can meet representatives from universities and colleges from all over the country who will tell you about their courses. You can also get information about career opportunities after courses. These are well worth attending, particularly if you have done a little work in advance, such as preparing questions. You will also be able to get information about grants and sponsorships.

Open Houses

Lists of open houses at universities and colleges should be available in your school. Some are for all students, others are for students interested in particular subjects. Ask your career counsellor or guidance counsellor for information.

"Taster" Courses

Some universities, colleges, and other organizations run courses of up to a week for interested students. Again, your school or local library will have information.

Reference Books

There are many reference books about higher education and the courses on offer. These will be available in your school library, in the career centre, or local public library. See page 115 for more details.

Moving On from Your Degree Course

Graduate Degrees and Professional Programs

Don't forget there are all sorts of different ways of getting advanced qualifications. They can be taken immediately after your first degree, but also later while you are at work or after some work experience. There are part-time as well as full-time programs.

Career Services Departments

Universities and colleges of higher education have career service offices where you can have access to an information library, computer databases, work opportunities information, and computer-aided and personal guidance from a career counsellor.

Career Fairs

Your career service office or department will organize presentations by employers about their companies, as well as general talks on career topics. There may also be career fairs, with many employers looking to recruit suitable graduates. This is where you can go and meet employers informally.

Summer Jobs

Science graduates are particularly successful at getting summer work, often in laboratories. This experience will give you a financial boost, and will also provide some insights into work roles and how you fit in at work.

Further Study

If you are interested in further academic study, talk to your professors. They will have many contacts with other departments and research groups, as well as information about grants and student loans.

Summary

Consider All Your Options

- Use your career library.
- Use computer databases.
- Use the Internet.
- Look at some of the resources on page 115.
- Visit conventions and science fairs.
- Go to open houses.
- Take introductory or "taster" courses in universities.

Decide What Really Matters to You

- Talk to your career/guidance counsellor.
- Talk to friends and family.

⊃ Talk to your teachers.

⊃ Gain some work experience or do some work shadowing.

⊃ Use computer-based guidance systems, such as CHOICES and *Discover*.

⊃ Talk to scientists you meet.

⊃ Keep reading magazines and watching TV programs.

Some Closing Thoughts

You will need to examine lots of different sources and talk to many different people. Try to relate the opinions you hear to the experiences of the people you are talking to. What is their standpoint? You will need other points of view to get a balanced picture. Allow for human error and then talk to a few more people.

You'll probably also want to think about how their information will affect you. Will you have the same experience? Do you have the same concerns? How will you avoid the pitfalls and make the best of the opportunities? Keep in mind that things are constantly changing.

You will meet helpful people to talk to through everyday student life, by using the career service office, through summer jobs and work experience, and through your friends, family, and relatives. Get in touch with professional associations and local firms. It is surprisingly easy to find the contacts. What takes more initiative is to ask people for some of their time and make good use of it.

You will find that most people will be happy to talk to you about their work and how they got into it. Sometimes the only problem is stopping them talking! If you are well prepared with questions on issues that are important for you, they will be glad to give you the time.

A word of warning: be wary of people who offer you directive advice. They are usually thinking of themselves, not you. Advice that begins, "If I were you..." usually means "I wish I had done this." They may be trying to be helpful, but the right decision for them would not necessarily suit you.

Whatever stage you're at, make yourself a plan of action. Make a list of things you have to do to get all the information, advice, and experience you need for a solid base for your next decision. Make a list and a timetable of actions. Then make sure you follow it up. It helps if you give yourself target dates and get a friend to check your progress. It's your future and only you can make the decisions, so put yourself firmly in charge.

And Finally...

This book has tried to give a positive but realistic picture of career opportunities with a science degree. An education in science is not a panacea for all. The bad news is that science has, in some respects, a poor image. Scientists often feel they have low status and that they get unfairly blamed for some of the problems of today. Research scientists are struggling for funding and a clear career structure, and many women scientists feel that science is still a man's world.

The good news, on the other hand, is that a science education will help you to understand and contribute to many of the most important issues of the 21st century. You will have knowledge, experience, and skills that can be applied in many different work situations, scientific and non-scientific, in Canada and abroad. You will be well-equipped to deal with the information technology revolution, and you will have an international outlook appropriate for the important challenges of the future. Together with other young science graduates, in all sorts of different roles, you can make a difference.

The final comment comes from a teacher of one of the most famous scientists of all time. It's worth remembering when you hit a difficult patch in your studies or career.

He will never amount to anything.

Albert Einstein's school report

GLOSSARY OF SCIENCE COURSES

This glossary gives a brief description of the main science degree subjects offered at universities and colleges. There are many other degree courses with variations on these titles. Sometimes this is because the course deals with a specialized branch or application of the subject, and sometimes the course approaches the subject in a particular way. For example, many degree courses have "applied" in their title. These courses usually cover much the same basic territory as the "pure" courses, but place more emphasis on the applications of the subject; they may also include periods of industrial or laboratory experience outside the university.

The title of a course is only a rough guide to what it actually covers. There can be wide variation in the content of courses with the same title and considerable overlap between courses with different titles. More complete information about individual courses is available from universities and colleges.

All university and college degree courses in science include some mathematics, statistics, and computer methods. Most courses also have practical laboratory work and, where appropriate, fieldwork; nearly all courses allow for extended project work in the later stages. Practical work is used to reinforce theoretical work as well as to teach practical techniques and experimental design.

Acoustics: the science of the production and transmission of sound, and its behaviour when it is reflected or absorbed by surfaces. Acoustic engineers are involved with both the enhancement of wanted sound and the suppression of sound that is unwanted or environmentally damaging. There are important applications in architecture and building construction, and in areas of mechanical engineering such as aeronautical and automotive engineering, as well as in the music and entertainment industries.

Agricultural Science/Agriculture: courses normally cover a mixture of the scientific, technological, practical, and business aspects of agriculture, although there is considerable variation in the emphasis given to each component. Some courses require students to have practical experience of agriculture before the course begins, and all have a strong practical element through laboratory and fieldwork projects. The science content is based on chemistry, biochemistry, and plant and animal biology. As the courses progress, topics with a more specific application to agriculture are introduced — for example, genetics and plant and animal breeding, animal nutrition and physiology, parasitology, and crop and soil science. Agriculture rapidly finds applications for new discoveries, so topics and specialized degrees in areas such as agricultural biotechnology are beginning to appear. Some specialized degree courses allow you to study a particular branch of agriculture such as crop or animal science, forestry or horticulture, or the business aspects. Other courses concentrate on a specific area of agricultural science, such as agricultural microbiology, usually with less emphasis on the practical farming content.

Agroforestry: the combined study of agriculture and forestry. As well as studying components of agriculture and forestry separately, there is emphasis on how mixed farming and forestry systems can be sustained in what are often environmentally sensitive areas.

Anatomy/Anatomical Sciences: the study of the structure of living organisms. (Although the term plant anatomy is widely used, degree courses in anatomy and anatomical sciences are concerned almost exclusively with mammalian anatomy and in some cases only with human anatomy.) Courses have changed over recent years with much less time devoted to the description of body structure (topographical anatomy). There is now much greater emphasis on the relationship between structure and function and on the way molecular and cellular structures determine macroscopic properties and structures, such as the organization and function of the body's systems. Specialized topics within anatomy include histology (the study of tissues), embryology (the study of development from the fertilized egg), pathology (the study of disease), and the comparative anatomy of different species.

Anatomy has links with biochemistry, physiology, genetics, and microbiology. Anatomy is also an important component of courses in medicine, dentistry, veterinary sciences, and most of the professions allied to medicine such as physiotherapy and radiography.

Animal Science: see zoology.

Arboriculture: the breeding and cultivation of trees and shrubs including planting, pruning, felling, prevention and treatment of diseases, and protection from pests. Degree courses in forestry include arboriculture as a major component.

Artificial Intelligence: the branch of computer science directed to the solution of problems normally associated with human intelligence. The range of the subject is very large — for example, it has links with psychology and linguistics — and a wide variety of techniques have been developed for specific application areas. These include trying to make computers understand natural human language, recognize and interpret visual scenes, acquire the knowledge and experience of human experts and then apply them to solving problems (these are called expert or knowledge-based systems), or learn from experience (one technique uses neural networks which mimic very crudely the way the brain is thought to work). Techniques in artificial intelligence led to the development of windowing interfaces found on personal computers. Artificial intelligence is a component of many computer science courses but can also be studied in specialist degrees.

Astronomy: the study of the universe and the matter it contains such as planets, stars and galaxies, the interstellar and intergalactic medium, comets, pulsars, quasars, and black holes. Branches of the subject include astrophysics and cosmology (the study of the universe as an ordered whole from its birth, through its evolution to its current state, to a variety of conjectured futures). The basis of the subject lies in physics and mathematics. A wide range of observational techniques are used, with electronic instrumentation and computer interpretation of data playing a major role. Astronomy is taught as a topic in physics degree courses and in specialist degrees. The astrophysics component of astronomy degree courses is often stressed by using the title "astronomy and astrophysics."

Astrophysics: the branch of astronomy concerned with using principles from physics to explain processes taking place in the universe. Examples of work done in astrophysics include explaining the production of energy in stars, the evolution of stars over their lifetime, the behaviour of pulsars, and the properties of quasars.

Biochemistry: the study of the chemistry of living organisms. The subject covers a very wide range of activity, including investigations into how an organism's metabolism is controlled, the way the nervous system and brain operate, the action of muscles, the role of hormones and how they control body function, and the operation of the immune system. A wide range of techniques is used to investigate biochemical reactions, both within the organism and in standard conditions in the laboratory. Techniques are also used to separate, purify, synthesize, and modify biomolecules. An important use of the last of these is in genetic engineering, where DNA is manipulated to alter the genetic properties of the organism.

Biochemistry has major applications in medicine, agriculture and — particularly since the development of biotechnology — a wide range of other industries including pharmaceuticals and the food industry. Biochemistry is also an important component in biology, chemistry, medicine, veterinary science, food science, pharmacology, and agricultural science degree courses.

Biology (Biological Science): the study of living organisms. Biology and biological science degree courses cover a wide range of topics, including plant and animal biology (botany and zoology), biochemistry, cell and molecular biology, genetics, and ecology. The vast range of the biological sciences, combined with the phenomenal progress that has been made in some areas, make it impossible to cover all of the subject in depth. Therefore, the later stages of most programs allow specialization in one or more of the branches just mentioned, or in more specialized topics such as pharmacology, physiology, immunology, toxicology, or microbiology. Work in areas such as biotechnology has recently opened up new potentials for the industrial application of biology. Greater awareness of environmental concerns has focused interest on the results produced by the study of ecology. Biology has links with agriculture, medicine, veterinary science, food science, and environmental science.

Biomedical Science: these courses cover the scientific basis of medicine and draw on many of the biological sciences. The subject is interdisciplinary, combining work in the biological and medical sciences. Courses usually begin by providing a basis in biochemistry, cell and molecular biology, and physiology. They build on this with more specialized study in areas such as pharmacology, genetics, nutrition, microbiology, immunology, pathology, neuroscience, and even biotechnology in some cases. These courses are a good preparation for work in the research laboratories of health and biologically related industries.

Biophysics: uses ideas and methods drawn originally from physics to study living organisms. Work in biophysics includes investigations at the macroscopic scale, such as the mechanics of skeletal and muscle action, but courses now concentrate much more on the cellular and molecular levels. For example, electronic instrumentation and computer data logging may be used to investigate the cell membrane. At the molecular level, X-ray crystallography, ultraviolet and infrared spectroscopy, and nuclear magnetic resonance are used to investigate and determine three-dimensional molecular structures. Some of these techniques have been adapted for medical use through, for example, computer-aided tomography (CAT scanners). Specialized medical biophysics courses are available. The courses are generally taught in association with other biology courses; the physics content is usually rather less than the biology content and is directed specifically towards biological applications.

Biotechnology: the application of biochemistry, molecular genetics, and microbiology to develop industrial processes based on biological activity. Biotechnology is an interdisciplinary subject drawing on the biological sciences (particularly biochemistry, microbiology, and genetics), chemistry, and chemical engineering, so courses cover aspects of all these, though the biological sciences tend to be the largest component. Biotechnology is a rapidly expanding area with great potential for many new and exciting applications in, for example, pharmaceuticals and medicine through the development of new drugs and medical treatments. It is now used in the chemicals industry, in agriculture through the use of genetic engineering to produce improved crops and livestock, and in the food industry, where brewing, for instance, represents an application of biotechnology that existed long before it became established as a separate discipline.

Botany (Plant/Crop Science): the study of plants or, in some cases, crops. Although botanists have traditionally been concerned mainly with the discovery and classification of new plants, the emphasis is now much more on general principles of cell and molecular biology, plant physiology, ecology, and conservation, though the emphasis given to each of these varies from program to program. Crop science courses are also concerned with practical issues affecting cultivation and protection from disease and pests. Despite the fact that the subject is one of the oldest sciences, new techniques such as cell culture and gene cloning mean that it continues to offer fresh and exciting challenges.

Cartography: see Mapping Science.

Cell Biology: the study of biology at the level of the cell, the fundamental unit of living organisms. Courses include work in biochemistry and molecular biology, common to nearly all biological science courses. However, they look in much greater detail at cell structure and function, cell membranes, the control, integration, and behaviour of cells in multicellular organisms, genetics at the cellular level (cytogenetics), and a variety of techniques such as cell culture.

Ceramic Science: the study of ceramics — hard, strong materials produced by firing mixtures containing clay. Familiar examples are pottery, bricks, and glazed tiles, but there are many other ceramic materials that are designed to have specific electrical, magnetic, and heat-resisting properties that give them a wide variety of industrial and other applications. A well-known example of the use of specialist ceramics is in the space shuttle's re-entry heat shield.

Chemistry: the study of the properties and reactions of the elements and their compounds. Although the traditional division of chemistry into physical, organic, and inorganic tends to be reflected in the organization of the initial stages of courses, the boundaries between them are not sharp. Specialized options, usually offered later in the courses, do not always fit neatly into this classification. The applications of chemistry are so broad and varied that chemists can be found working in nearly all parts of industry, including obvious areas such as chemicals and pharmaceuticals, as well as less obvious ones such as the food industry and wherever materials are produced or processed (for example, in the steel and ceramics industries).

Chemists also work in the public sector in analytical laboratories monitoring health and safety. They are at the forefront in the fight against environmental problems; for example, it is chemists who have to find effective alternatives to environmentally harmful substances such as CFCs.

Chemistry program usually provide opportunities to specialize late in the program. However, there are also more specialized degrees, such as biological, medicinal, and environmental chemistry, which concentrate on one particular area, though they usually build from a solid foundation in general chemistry.

Chiropody (Podiatry): the diagnosis, treatment, and management of conditions affecting the foot and lower limbs. Clinical practice is an important part of all courses and can occupy up to half of the time. Theoretical work covers the structure and function of the normal limb, the biomechanics of locomotion and gait, pathology, podiatric medicine, behavioural science, and treatment techniques. Qualified chiropodists work in both hospitals and private practice.

Computer Science/Studies: the study of the principles and use of computers. Courses vary greatly, some taking a scientific/mathematical approach, others concentrating on the practical uses of computers. Many courses have a hardware component covering basic logic circuit design and computer architectures, though more specialized topics such as VLSI (very large scale integrated circuits) design may also be available as options. The purpose of the hardware component is usually to give a background for other parts of the course. Courses in electronics or electronic engineering may be more suitable for professional training as a hardware engineer. The largest amount of time is usually devoted to work on software. All courses cover at least one programming language, and some considerably more, as well as operating systems (the programs used by computers to control their hardware and to run the user's programs), though the depth to which the underlying principles of operating systems are covered will vary. The greatest variation between courses comes from the way they treat applications software. Some concentrate on the low-level software engineering aspects of producing applications, others more on their use in particular areas such as for business information systems.

Artificial intelligence is a major area of computer science, which some courses cover in considerable depth. They may cover both the basic theory, some of which is drawn from psychology and linguistics, and the use of specific techniques such as expert systems (also called knowledge-based systems) or neural networks.

Courses vary considerably in how much formal theory they include and the depth to which they go. The theory has been developed in an attempt to help programmers produce "correct" programs (in the sense that they behave as intended in all circumstances). The need for this arises from the fact that only very small programs can be tested exhaustively. The theory uses ideas and notation drawn from mathematics; in its more advanced forms it is highly mathematical.

Crop Science: see Botany.

Cybernetics: the study of systems and how they are controlled. Applications include industrial automation and robotics. Techniques are drawn from a wide area including electronics, computer science, artificial intelligence, and instrumentation.

Dentistry: dentists work to conserve their patients' teeth and to treat problems of decay, gum disease, and misalignment if they arise. The courses involve considerable clinical practice. The basic content of all courses is very similar, but they differ in the way it is organized, with emphasis given to different elements and the possibilities for elective studies in the later stages of the course.

Dietetics: the study of diet and nutrition. Courses with "dietetics" in their title usually provide a period of professional training in hospitals. Dieticians also work in the food industry and in private practice. Courses include components of physiology, biochemistry, and microbiology, together with elements drawn from the behavioural and social sciences.

Earth Science: an interdisciplinary subject combining the study of geology (the largest component) with aspects of physical geography and, in some cases, oceanography, meteorology, and climatology.

Ecology: the study of the interrelationships between plants and animals, and between them and their environment. It looks at how the environment influences and is influenced by individual organisms, populations of an individual species, and communities of different species. Ecology is normally taught alongside other biological science courses and often shares with them a basic grounding in topics such as plant and animal biology, cell and molecular biology, and genetics. Issues of conservation and environmental damage through pollution and other factors are usually covered. The later stages of programs often allow some specialization in the study of specific ecosystems, such as marine, freshwater, or agricultural ecology.

As well as being available as a specialist degree subject, ecology is taught in many biological science courses. It is also a major component in environmental science courses with a biological science orientation, though ecology courses generally give less emphasis to social and policy issues.

Electronics: the study of the construction and use of electronic devices. These devices are now almost exclusively semiconductor-based. Courses usually give a balanced treatment of both linear (analogue) and digital electronics. A wide range of applications is normally covered from areas such as instrumentation, control systems, computer design and architecture, and audio-electronics.

Environmental Health: courses are concerned with the health implications of environmental factors such as food safety, pollution, and noise. Courses cover the relevant basic science such as microbiology, anatomy, and environmental studies, as well as more specific topics such as food safety and hygiene, and occupational health and safety. They also cover the relevant legislation and how it is enforced. Qualified environmental health officers work mainly for local authorities to improve standards of health and safety, particularly in food production and service, but also in other aspects of people's living and working environments.

Environmental Science/Studies: an interdisciplinary subject studying the environment and the very wide range of factors affecting it. The content and emphasis of courses vary considerably. Some courses have a physical sciences (most particularly, chemistry) or earth science orientation; rather more have a biological sciences bias and others a balance of approaches, though in the latter case options may allow some specialization in a particular area. Many of the courses with a biological orientation may share appreciable content with courses in ecology, but tend to be more concerned with practical and social issues, and the resulting consequences for policy. This means that many courses also include relevant aspects of law, economics, and other social sciences. There is a wide variety of courses specializing in specific aspects of the subject, such as environmental management, environmental chemistry, environmental biology, or environmental toxicology (pollution).

Ergonomics: the study of people in their working environment, and in particular the design of working practices, equipment, and tools for optimum efficiency and protection of workers' health and safety. Courses include relevant aspects of anatomy, psychology, physiology, industrial engineering, and design. Issues dealt with include furniture design, factory and office lay-out, and environmental conditions such as heating and lighting.

Food Science/Studies: the scientific study of food, including production, processing, storage, and distribution, as well as nutrition. Food science courses are firmly based on chemistry and biochemistry, with contributions from microbiology and physiology. Food studies courses usually have a less intensive science content and give more emphasis to the general aspects of food such as related economic and social issues. Both types of program include topics relevant to management in the food industry. However, some specialized courses dealing with business aspects of the food industry, such as food marketing, often include some work in food science.

Forestry: courses cover all aspects of the cultivation and management of forests. Building on a foundation of basic science including chemistry, geology, botany, zoology, and soil science, courses cover more specialized topics such as wood structure, tree and forest husbandry (silviculture), tree pests and diseases, forest measurement, land use and urban forestry, together with economics and management. There is a strong emphasis on practical work, as well as commercial and technical aspects.

Genetics: the study of the inheritable characteristics of organisms. Genetics evolved through the study of the development of genetic variation in whole populations, sometimes over long periods. Although this still plays a part, the emphasis of courses is now much more at the cellular and molecular level, where an understanding of the structure of DNA and the way it can be manipulated allows the possibility of changing the genetic make-up of organisms through the techniques of genetic engineering. The scientific, medical, and commercial applications of these techniques are immense and only just beginning to be realized. Programs in human genetics often cover the topic of genetic counselling, which requires technical, social, and personal skills.

Geochemistry: the chemistry of rocks and the processes occurring during rock formation and transformation. Chemistry is an important tool for the geologist, providing both a method of identification through analysis and the means for explaining many of the properties of rocks and the processes taking place during their formation. Geochemistry is therefore often an important component of geology courses, but specialist courses are also available allowing for deeper treatment of the subject. Geochemical prospecting is used commercially to find deposits of ores from analyses of soils, water courses, and sediments.

Geology: the study of the Earth, including its composition, structure, and historical development. Geology courses draw on a wide range of basic sciences and cover many different topics including crystallography, mineralogy, and petrology (the study of rock origin, composition, structure, and alteration), geochemistry, geophysics, stratigraphy (the study of strata laid down over time), and paleontology (the study of fossils). The applications of geology to oil and mineral prospecting and extraction are obvious, but it is also important in civil engineering projects, such as tunnel boring and the building of dams and reservoirs. A knowledge of the geology of the area is also important for the analysis of environmental problems, such as the flow of pollutants from ground water to water courses or drinking water.

Geophysics: the study of the physical properties of the Earth (and, by extension, other planets). By studying these properties, geophysicists are able to infer the structure of the Earth and the nature of processes within it at great depths beneath the surface. Geophysicists draw on a wide range of physics, including theories of fluid and heat flow, electromagnetism, gravitation, and wave propagation through solids and fluids. Data are gathered using sophisticated electronic instruments, including satellites and space probes. Computers are used extensively to control instruments, process data, and then interpret it through the use of complex mathematical models. Geophysicists make a major contribution to the search for oil and minerals. They are also involved in work on earthquakes, which may in time enable them to give reliable predictions of when and where they will occur. Geophysics topics appear in most geology and some physics courses.

Health Studies: this area covers a variety of different courses where biological and medical subjects are combined with social studies, health administration, and in some courses sports management and administration. The courses are often part of combined or modular degrees with a wide choice of options.

Horticulture: the cultivation of plants for food (commercial horticulture) or to enhance the environment (amenity horticulture). Programs begin with a foundation in basic science usually including botany/plant science, biochemistry, soil science, ecology, and genetics. They then introduce more specialist horticultural topics such as plant production, plant pests and diseases, crop protection, landscape management, and the use of organic methods. All courses place strong emphasis on practical work and prominence is given to commercial as well as technical aspects throughout. There is usually a wide range of options in the final year and it is often possible to specialize in commercial or amenity horticulture at that stage. Horticulture has links with the biological sciences, forestry, and agriculture.

Information Science: the study of the selection, acquisition, organization, storage, retrieval, and dissemination of information. Information science courses provide professional qualifications in librarianship. The courses contain topics such as classification systems that are directed specifically to library work, but much attention is also directed towards the creation and use of computer-based information systems. This means that the programs are now less distinct from other programs directed at the information industry, such as information management, information systems, and information technology.

Information Technology: this title is used for two rather different types of computing programs. The first type has an engineering orientation with more emphasis on hardware, particularly in connection with communications and networks, than is usual in computer science courses. The second type of course is concerned mainly with the use of business or management software systems, with less emphasis on low-level programming and hardware than in most computer science courses. Courses with titles such as Business Information Technology are usually of this second type, but in general the only way of telling the orientation of a specific course is from a detailed description of its contents.

Linguistics: the scientific study of language and its structure. This includes how sounds are used to make speech (phonetics and phonology), how sentences are constructed (syntax), how meaning is conveyed using words and sentences (semantics), and how language is used in context (pragmatics). Linguistics is also a component of some courses in foreign languages, speech science, education, computer science (particularly artificial intelligence), and psychology.

Mapping Science (Cartography): the study of the processes required for the creation of maps. The process of creating a map can be divided into data acquisition, analysis, and presentation. One aspect of data acquisition is surveying, which includes land-based and remote sensing using aerial and satellite imaging. However, since maps are used to display a wide range of information, including such things as market research results, data acquisition also includes issues such as social survey and sampling techniques. The analysis phase includes image analysis and processing, as well as statistical analysis. The presentation stage covers a wide range from manual mapping to the construction of computer-based geographical information systems. Mapping science is often a component of degrees in surveying, geography, and geology.

Marine Biology: the study of the biological systems found in the sea, including individual organisms and a variety of ecosystems. The courses build from a solid foundation in biological science, covering basic plant and animal biology, cell biology, biochemistry, genetics, and evolution. An understanding of the marine environment is gained through the study of physical, chemical, and atmospheric processes within and around the seas and oceans. This work is enhanced with more specialized courses in topics such as the physiology of marine organisms, food chain processes, behaviour, marine pollution, conservation, fisheries, and aquaculture. See also Oceanography.

Materials Science: the study of the physical properties of natural and synthetic materials used in industry and construction. Many of the advances that have led to an increase in the standard of living this century have been brought about by a greater understanding of the way materials can be used and by the introduction of new materials that have improved properties and are cheaper to produce. For example, much of the engineering industry relies on the use of high-performance alloys. Courses cover a wide range of materials, which may include natural materials such as wood or stone, though the emphasis is more commonly on artificial or processed materials such as ceramics, metals, semiconductors, and plastics. The subject is very active and promises exciting developments — for example, the production of new semiconductors offering greatly enhanced computer performance and the recent development of high-temperature superconductors. Programs draw from a variety of other subjects but are principally based on solid-state physics and chemistry. Some programs allow the specialized study of individual materials later in the course and others from the beginning. Materials science is also a major part of materials engineering degree programs and is often a component of mechanical engineering programs.

Mathematics: a diverse subject, but one that is developing more rapidly now than at any time in the past. There are some broad divisions within the subject, which you can concentrate on by taking a specialist degree or by taking options in a general mathematics degree. Pure mathematics includes topics such as calculus, algebra, and geometry, though the content of the last two in particular is markedly different from what is taught in secondary school. It also includes topics that are less familiar, such as logic, ring and field theory, number theory, and topology. Applied mathematics includes topics such as mechanics, electromagnetic field theory, fluid mechanics, relativity and quantum theory, and elementary particle physics. Applicable mathematics includes a variety of techniques that are used widely in business and covers topics in statistics and methods of optimization such as linear programming. Statistics is also a component of many mathematics courses. Virtually all courses include some computer science. There are many specialist mathematics courses dealing with particular application areas, such as business mathematics or mathematical physics. All science and engineering courses include some mathematics.

Medical Laboratory Science: the science used in hospital medical laboratories to aid in diagnosis and treatment. Programs begin with a foundation of biochemistry, microbiology and cell and molecular biology, before introducing the more specialized topics such as medical biochemistry (for the analysis of body fluids), hematology (the study of blood), histology (the study of cells, particularly for cancer diagnosis), and immunology (for detecting antibodies and tissue typing). The courses are also good preparation for work in the research laboratories of health and biologically related industries. Medical laboratory science has links with biology, biochemistry, and medicine.

Medical Physics: the study of the interaction between the body and all types of radiation used for diagnostic and therapeutic purposes. Diagnostic techniques include X-rays, ultrasound scans, gamma-ray imaging, and magnetic resonance imaging. Therapeutic techniques include laser surgery and radiation treatment. Programs start with a foundation of mathematics and physics, including electromagnetism, atomic physics, nuclear physics, and optical physics. This is built on with more specialized topics such as biophysics, physiological medicine, and radiography.

Medicine: programs leading to professional qualification as a physician or surgeon. They begin with a foundation in basic medical science subjects lasting about two years. The topics covered include human anatomy and physiology, biochemistry, microbiology, pharmacology, genetics, immunology, and pathology. The remainder of the program is devoted to clinical training, though some formal teaching continues throughout this period. Programs often contain an elective period toward the end when students can broaden their experience by performing a research project or gaining clinical experience in a new environment such as in a foreign country. At the end of the program, an internship of a least one year is required. This is followed by a residency, the length of which depends on the specialty chosen.

Metallurgy: the study of the extraction, purification, production, and properties of metals. Metals play a vital part in all areas of industry, especially in areas such as engineering and construction. Metallurgists ensure that metals have the correct properties to perform the task required effectively and safely. They create high-performance alloys for special purposes in industries such as aerospace, as well as ensuring, for instance, that the quality of steel used in car manufacturing is consistent. Metallurgy courses draw on knowledge from a wide range of other subjects including chemistry, physics, geology, and crystallography. Metallurgy is also available as part of materials science/engineering courses, and has links with mechanical and other engineering degrees.

Meteorology: the study of the weather and atmospheric processes. The behaviour of the atmosphere is extremely complex and meteorologists have to draw on a wide range of information, techniques, and theories. The meteorologist uses acquired knowledge to build sophisticated mathematical models and computer simulations to understand and predict evolving weather patterns. Courses include physics and mathematics, as well as topics such as atmospheric dynamics, atmospheric physics, climate change, surface processes, and oceanography.

Microbiology: the study of micro-organisms including bacteria, viruses, protozoa, and certain algae and fungi. The courses are often taught alongside other biological science courses and often share with them a basic grounding in topics such as plant and animal biology, biochemistry, cell and molecular biology, genetics, and ecology. This leads to more specialized topics such as bacteriology, virology, mycology (the study of fungi), and immunology. Programs often have a range of options related to the application of microbiology to agriculture and medicine. The importance of microbes as agents of disease has long been recognized, but the explosion of interest in biotechnology in recent years has given extra impetus to the study of microbiology. For example, bacteria can be genetically engineered so that they produce human enzymes or hormones. The bacteria can then be grown on an industrial scale to produce these compounds commercially for medical use. Microbiology is also available as a component of degrees in biological sciences, medicine, veterinary science, dentistry, horticulture, and agriculture.

Molecular Biology: the study of the structure and reactions of large biological molecules such as nucleic acids and proteins. The courses are often taught alongside other biological science courses and often share with them a basic grounding in topics such as chemistry, biochemistry, plant and animal biology, cell biology, and genetics. Other topics that may be taught later in the program include microbiology, immunology, and biotechnology. Molecular biology is at the centre of many of the most exciting developments in biology and its influence has spread to many other branches of the subject such as genetics. The scientific, medical, and commercial applications of genetic engineering have created even greater interest in the subject. Molecular biology is often combined with cell biology and is also available as a component of degrees in biological science, biochemistry, and agriculture.

Neuroscience: the study of the nervous system including the brain. Neuroscience draws on a wide range of other biological and medical subjects from molecular biology at the smallest level, through the chemical and electrical communications between cells (cell biology), to the behaviour of the whole organism (psychology). Because of this, the programs normally begin with a solid foundation of biochemistry, animal biology, cell and molecular biology, pharmacology, and physiology. Understanding the function of the brain is one of the most challenging problems in modern biology and medicine, with many potential applications.

Nursing Studies: degree courses that include nursing training but enhanced to a degree-level qualification. Some programs extend the depth of nursing subjects and are based in science/medical faculties. Others extend the breadth and offer more social sciences such as sociology, psychology, economics, health policy, and health studies. Some have a balance of these approaches. All programs cover anatomy, physiology, pharmacology, human development, nursing techniques, and practical training, and most include some management studies. Some degree programs offer specialization in the final year in, for example, mental health, care of children, care of the elderly, or care of those with learning difficulties.

Nutrition: the study of the body's requirements for food and how they can be met. The courses are often similar to and taught with courses in dietetics, except that they do not have a period of professional practice. There are also a number of courses in animal nutrition which are taught alongside agricultural sciences. Nutrition can also be studied as part of courses in physiology, food science, and agriculture.

Occupational Health and Safety: the study of health and safety at work and in the wider environment and how they can be maintained and improved. Subjects studied include biochemistry, physiology, ergonomics, occupational health, environmental measurement methods, toxicology, law, and risk management. These programs provide specialized training for jobs in health and safety advice and inspection.

Occupational Therapy: courses provide professional training for occupational therapists. Qualified occupational therapists are employed in hospitals to help people overcome the effects of mental or physical illnesses or disability, so that they can live as full and independent lives as possible. The programs cover human biology, psychology, anatomy, and physiology, as well as the principles and techniques of treatment. All the courses include practical work with patients suffering from physical and/or psychological difficulties or disabilities, and draw on personal and social skills as well as technical knowledge.

Oceanography: the scientific study of the oceans. Oceanography is a very broad subject drawing on many other subjects. For example, understanding the intricate patterns of ocean currents, tides, and waves requires complex computer models drawing on theories of fluid flow from physics and mathematics. Studies of the sea floor apply knowledge from geology. Marine chemists study interactions at the interfaces between sea water and materials in the seabed, and sea water and the atmosphere at the surface. Marine biologists investigate all aspects of life in the sea. The practical importance of understanding the oceans is immense. For instance, the oceans have been used to absorb vast amounts of waste material, and only with a proper understanding of processes within the ocean can the resulting risks be assessed. The oceans are a major food resource and support major transport systems. Oil is already being taken from below the seabed and there is potential for extracting other materials. The oceans also have a major effect on climate. Oceanography can also be studied as part of a course in earth science or geophysics.

Optometry (Ophthalmic Optics): courses provide professional training for optometrists (also called ophthalmic opticians). Optometrists carry out eye tests to detect abnormalities and vision defects, analyze the results, and prescribe and dispense corrective lenses.

Optometrists also carry out work in orthoptics, checking for diseases of the eye such as glaucoma, and referring patients to specialist doctors (ophthalmic surgeons) for treatment. Courses include the anatomy and physiology of the eye, optics, clinical optometry (measurement), methods of examination and diseases of the eye, as well as clinical work with patients. They also draw on personal and social skills and technical knowledge.

Orthoptics: the diagnosis and treatment of disorders of the eyes caused by problems with the muscles controlling the eye. The courses provide professional training in orthoptics. Much of the work is with young children but orthoptists also work with adults suffering from a variety of conditions such as the after-effects of accidents and strokes. Orthoptists can treat some of the problems they diagnose, but refer more severe cases to specialist doctors (ophthalmic surgeons). The courses include the anatomy and physiology of the eye, optics, child development, and ophthalmology (the scientific study of the eye). The courses also include clinical work with patients and draw on personal and social skills as well as technical knowledge.

Pathology: the study of disease and disease-causing micro-organisms such as bacteria and viruses. It includes the study of microscopic and macroscopic changes in the organization of tissues, and chemical changes in tissues and body fluids. The programs start with the study of healthy organisms and progress to contrasting them with those affected by disease. Anatomy, physiology, cell biology, genetics, and microbiology, as well as more specialized topics such as cell pathology and hematology (the study of the structure, function, and diseases of blood), are included in courses.

Pharmacology: the study of the action of drugs on living systems. Programs build from a foundation of chemistry, biochemistry, cell and molecular biology, physiology, and pathology. In addition, there are specialist topics such as the mechanisms of drug action and drug toxicity. Pharmacologists are involved in medical research and play a vital role in the pharmaceuticals industry, helping with the development and screening of new drugs for use in medicine, veterinary science, and agriculture.

Pharmacy: programs provide professional training for pharmacists. About one-third of the programs is spent studying pharmacology. The rest of the time is used to study basic subjects such as chemistry and microbiology, as well as more specialized topics such as pharmaceutical chemistry (the structural analysis and synthesis of drugs), pharmaceutics (the manufacture of drugs and their formulation into a suitable form for humans or animals), and clinical pharmacology (the study of the effects of drugs on the human body). Other subjects that may be studied include toxicology (the study of poisons) and pharmaceutical engineering.

Physics: the science concerned with the behaviour and properties of matter and energy, but largely excluding those processes involving a change in chemical composition. Physics encompasses investigations at the smallest possible scale of sub-elementary particles called quarks, as well as explanations of the origin and evolution of the entire universe using general relativity. Indeed, attempts are now being made to explain both these extremes within a single unified theory. However, even if such a theory is developed, there will still be many challenging fundamental problems left for the physicist in areas such as low-temperature physics, solid-state physics, plasma physics, and astrophysics to name just a few, as well as in other areas where the techniques of physics are used, such as medical physics and geophysics.

Programs usually build from a solid foundation of classical physics covering topics such as mechanics, electromagnetism, properties of matter, thermodynamics, and statistical mechanics. To these are added quantum mechanics and relativity, which were developed in the early years of the 20th century and revolutionized the way physicists and others viewed the world. In the later stages of programs, more specialized topics can usually be studied, such as nuclear physics, astronomy, astrophysics, biophysics, geophysics, X-ray crystallography, medical physics, elementary particle physics, electronics, and laser physics. Mathematics is also an important component of all physics courses, particularly those with options in theoretical physics. Physics topics are also studied within all engineering courses, electronics and applied mathematics.

Physiology: the study of how animals function. (Plant physiology appears as a title for topics in botany and biological science courses, but you can assume that courses called physiology are only concerned with animal, and often just vertebrate, physiology.) Physiology covers all levels, from the subcellular (such as the operation of cell membranes), through the function of individual organs (such as the way the heart operates), to the way the animal functions as a whole. In explaining how organisms function, physiology draws on ideas and techniques from a wide range of other subjects including physics, chemistry, and many of the biological sciences such as anatomy, biochemistry, genetics, pharmacology, and microbiology. Physiology can also be studied within programs in biological science, human biology, and agriculture, and is an important component of courses in medicine, dentistry, veterinary science, and most of the professions allied to medicine such as physiotherapy and radiography.

Physiotherapy: courses provide professional training for physiotherapists. Qualified physiotherapists work in hospitals and the community. They use physical methods including manipulation, massage, infra-red heat treatment, and remedial exercises to treat clients of all ages who may be suffering from any of a wide range of disabilities and disorders, such as arthritis, mental illness, stroke, and accidents. Courses include anatomy, physiology, pathology, human science, biomechanics, and treatment techniques. All the courses include clinical work with clients and draw on personal and social skills as well as technical knowledge.

Plant Science: see Botany.

Podiatry: see Chiropody.

Polymer Science: the study of polymers (molecules made up of long chains of repeating units), including their formation, properties, and uses. Polymeric materials come in many different forms such as plastics, fibres, and foams; they may be synthetic, such as nylon or polystyrene, or natural such as rubber or cellulose. It is possible to fine-tune the properties of polymers in the manufacturing process, so they can often be adapted for different applications. They can also be combined with other materials to form composites that display the best properties of each material. The courses are specialized materials science courses. They are often taught alongside other materials science courses and share some common content. Polymer science can also be studied as a component of programs in materials science and chemistry, though the approach in the latter will be rather different.

Psychology: the scientific study of the mind. It is a very broad subject and different programs may emphasize very different aspects of the subject. One reflection of this is that it may be offered as a B.Sc. within a science or social science faculty or a B.A. within an arts faculty. (If they are offered at the same institution, much of the teaching may be common, with the main differences being the options offered.) Programs also vary in the amount of work on animals, as well as in the emphasis given to different branches of psychology such as experimental psychology, cognitive psychology (the study of thought processes, memory, and language), physiological psychology (the study of the relationship between brain function and psychological processes), comparative psychology (the study of animal behaviour and the similarities and differences between species), developmental psychology (changes in psychological processes during maturation into adulthood), social psychology (how people and animals behave in groups), the psychology of individual differences (the study of factors such as personality and intelligence), abnormal psychology (the study of abnormal behaviour), and applied psychology (the application of psychology to practical problems, such as in negotiation strategies). Psychology can also be studied in a wide variety of other programs including education, medicine, and the professions allied to medicine such as nursing and occupational therapy.

Radiography: programs provide professional training in diagnostic or therapeutic radiography. (The two branches of the profession are distinct and the courses are separate, though some teaching may be common to both.) Diagnostic radiographers work in the X-ray departments of hospitals or in health centres. They use a wide variety of techniques, including X-rays, ultrasound, magnetic resonance imaging, and computer-aided tomography to produce images to help doctors diagnose illness. Therapeutic radiographers work in hospital clinical oncology (cancer) departments. They plan and administer treatment using a variety of radiation sources such as X-rays and radioactive isotopes. Both types of programs include anatomy, physiology, pathology, radiographic physics, radiographic techniques, patient care, and professional practice as radiographers. All the courses include clinical work with patients and draw on personal and social skills as well as technical knowledge.

Speech Sciences/Speech Therapy: the study of speech, including the anatomy and physiology of the mouth and throat, phonetics (vocal sounds), linguistics (the structure of language), psychology, and the pathology of speech problems. Other topics covered include acoustics, audiology, neurology, and education. Speech therapy courses also include clinical practice and contribute to a professional qualification in the diagnoses and treatment of speech defects. Speech therapists work with children in schools and clinics and with adults with speech problems, such as stroke patients.

Statistics: the science of collecting and analyzing numerical data. Statistics is a major branch of mathematics with applications in practically every area of scientific, commercial, and administrative activity. Programs cover a range of basic mathematical subjects such as calculus and algebra, as well as more specialized topics such as probability analysis, statistical distributions, and a wide range of statistical analysis techniques. The use of computers is essential for the statistician, so programs include numerical analysis and computer science, with particular emphasis on the use of a wide range of software packages for statistical analysis in various fields. Statistics can also be studied in combination with mathematics or as part of a mathematics degree. Topics in statistics are also taught in all science and medical degree courses and form important components of courses in the social sciences, such as psychology and business studies.

Veterinary Sciences: programs provide professional training in veterinary medicine and include many similar subjects to medical degrees, such as anatomy, biochemistry, physiology, medicine, surgery, obstetrics, pharmacology, and pathology — though the focus is naturally on animals rather than humans. Courses cover large animal (farm livestock) and small animal (domestic pets) practice, as well as some exotic animals. Practical clinical training is a major component of all courses and dominates the second half of the program. It is usually carried out in clinics attached to the veterinary school and by internships with practicing veterinarians. Experience of practical work with livestock on a farm is also part of the training.

Zoology/Animal Science: the scientific study of animals including their anatomy, physiology, classification, distribution, behaviour, and ecology. Programs often run alongside other courses in biological science and share with them a foundation in biochemistry, cell and molecular biology, microbiology, and genetics. Many courses stress the practical importance of zoology, with specialist topics such as fisheries biology and parasitology. In fact, some animal science courses are directed specifically towards agricultural applications.

Zoology can also be studied as a component of courses in biological science, agriculture, and environmental science.

RESOURCE LIST

Remember, the publications on this list are just a starting point. There is a great deal of information available from a huge variety of sources such as university and college calendars, career centres, the Internet, newspapers and magazines, television and radio programs, your parents, friends, relatives, career/guidance counsellors, teachers, your school or university library, public libraries, and so on. Just ask!

Choosing a Science Degree

The Complete Guide to Canadian Universities, Self-Counsel Press

Directory of Canadian Universities, Association of Universities and Colleges of Canada

The Macleans' Guide to Universities

Your Guide to Canadian Colleges, Self-Counsel Press

Graduate Programs

Peterson's Graduate Programs in Engineering and Applied Sciences, Peterson's Guides, Inc.

Peterson's Graduate Programs in the Biological and Agricultural Sciences, Peterson's Guides, Inc.

Peterson's Graduate Programs in the Physical Sciences and Mathematics, Peterson's Guides, Inc.

The *Peterson's* guides give information on graduate and professional programs offered by accredited colleges and universities in the United States and accredited colleges, universities, and institutions in Canada, Mexico, Europe, and Africa that are accredited by U.S. accrediting bodies.

Postgraduate Study Abroad, published by UNESCO

Careers with a Science Degree

Nicholas Basta. *The Environmental Career Guide*, Wiley and Sons.

Job Choices in Science and Engineering, National Association of Colleges and Employers.

National Occupational Classification: classifies about 500 occupational groups according to skill level.

Occupational Profiles: published by Alberta Advanced Education and Career Development, outlining responsibilities, working conditions, qualifications, employment and advancement, salary, and other sources of information.

Working and Studying Abroad

⊃   *The Canadian Guide to Working and Living Overseas*, Intercultural Systems.

⊃   Griffiths, Susan. *Teaching English Abroad*, Vacation Work.

⊃   *What in the World Is Going On?* Canadian Bureau for International Education (CBIE)

General Science Interest

The Cartoon Guide to Physics, HarperCollins, 1992.

Davies, Paul. *The Mind of God*, Touchstone, 1993.

Grace, Eric. *Biotechnology Unzipped: Promises & Realities*, Trifolium Books Inc., 1997.

Todoroff, Cindy. *Presenting Science with Impact: Presentation Skills for Guide for Scientists, Medical Researchers & Health Care Professionals*, Trifolium Books Inc., 1997.

James Watson. *The Double Helix*, Penguin, 1970.

Career Development

Beck, Nuala. *Shifting Gears*, HarperCollins, Toronto, 1992.

Bolles, Richard. *What Color is Your Parachute?* A practical manual for job hunters and career changers. Berkeley, California: Ten Speed Press, annual.

Bolt, Laurence. *Zen and the Art of Making a Living*, Penguin, 1993.

Career Connections Series. Toronto/Calgary: Trifolium Books Inc./Weigl Educational Publishers (1993-1996)

> *Great Careers for People Interested in Living Things*
>
> *Great Careers for People Interested in The Human Body*
>
> *Great Careers for People Interested in Math & Computers*
>
> *Great Careers for People Interested in How Things Work*
>
> *Great Careers for People Who Like Being Outdoors*
>
> *Great Careers for People Concerned About the Environment*
>
> *Great Careers for People Interested in Film, Video, & Photography*
>
> *Great Careers for People Who Life to Work With Their Hands*
>
> *Great Careers for People Interested in Communications Technology*

Lang, Jim. *Make Your Own Breaks: Become an Entrepreneur & Create Your Own Future*, Trifolium Books Inc., Toronto, 1994.

Radical Change in the World of Work: The Workbook, Alberta Advanced Education and Career Development.

Robert, Wayne. *Get a Life: Make a Buck, Dance Around the Dinosaurs and Save the World While You're at It.*, Toronto, 1995.

Worzel, Richard. *Facing the Future*, Stoddart, Toronto, 1994.

APPENDIX 1

Some Helpful Addresses and Websites

Association of Professional Engineers and Geoscientists of British Columbia
200-4010 Regent St.,
Burnaby, British Columbia V5C 6N2
(http://www.apeg.bc.ca)

Canadian Centre for Creative Technology,
8 Yonge Street East,
Waterloo, Ontario N2J 2L3

Canadian Federation of Biological Societies (CFBS)
104-1750 Courtwood Cres.,
Ottawa, Ontario K2C 2B5
(http://www.hwc.ca:8080/cfbs)

Canadian Fitness and Lifestyle Research Institute,
201-185 Somerset St., W.,
Ottawa, Ontario, K2P 0J2
(http://activeliving.ca/activeliving/cflri.html)

Canadian Industrial Innovation Centre,
156 Columbia Street West,
Waterloo, Ontario N2L 3L3
(http://www.innovationcentre.ca)

Canadian Museums Association,
289 Metcalfe Street, Suite 400,
Ottawa, Ontario K2P 1R7

Canadian Science Writers' Association (CSWA)
P.O. Box 75, Stn. A,
Toronto, Ontario M5W 1A2
(http://www.interlog.com/~cswa)

Canadian Society of Laboratory Technologists
P.O.Box 2830, LCD 1,
Hamilton, Ontario L8N 3N8
(905) 528-8642

Institute for Space and Terrestrial Science
4850 Keele St.,
North York, Ontario M3J 3K1
(http://www.ists.ca)

The Natural Sciences and Engineering Research Council of Canada,
Constitution Square, Tower II,
350 Albert St.,
Ottawa, Ontario K1A 1H5
(http://www.nserc.ca)

Some Useful Websites

www.ngr.schoolnet.ca/sites/career_c/

This site offers a choice of materials for students, parents, and teachers. There are a number of career development and search materials (more every month). One very helpful feature is the sequence of personal management activities. Try them a number of times over a year to see how your interests may have changed.

www.infoweb.magi.com/~ccdffcac/cgcf/careerlinks.html

This is the Canadian Career Development Foundation's "Other Career Links" site. Use it as a link to CanWorkNet, SchoolNet, Trifolium Books, and others.

www.schoolnet.ca/ngr

This is the National Graduate Register, an on-line resume database available to employers, as well as on-line job postings that can be accessed by students. Students can use their college or university password to post material on the service, but there is quite of bit of information that anyone can access. For example, you can link to the Experience Canada program, a 6-month program that gives students work experience and training outside of their home province or territory.

www.cacee.com

This is Canada's On-line Campus Career Centre, maintained by the Canadian Association of Career Educators and Employer WorkWeb. You will find job search advice, links to other career sites, such as colleges and university career centres, and employers.

www.monster.com

This is an international job posting service that you can use to research over 4,000 companies using updated descriptions (an option is to use a map to start your search by location). There is a free "job search agent" named "Jobbo the Hunt" that can identify potential jobs by location, type, and area of interest.

www.careeredge.org

Career Edge is an internship program that is sponsored by private industry to help graduates who are looking for employment to find a company that needs their skills. The program matches graduating students who have no relevant job experience with companies willing to offer internships.

www.cybf.ca

A corporate initiative (the Canadian Youth Business Foundation) designed to help young people set up and succeed at their own businesses.

www.experiencecanada.com

This school-to-work transition program is a federal government initiative to help graduates who have not been able to find jobs. It emphasizes citizenship and community life, as well as employability. Check it out.

APPENDIX 2

The National Occupational Classification (NOC)

This system, developed by the federal government, divides occupations into occupational groups. Within each group, the level of skill required to do the job decreases from professional to unskilled. The complete NOC is available in high schools, college, universities, and most libraries in book form, providing valuable information on each occupational group, including the skills required to enter and do the job and the education and training needed to be successful. Check for it on-line as well.

Note: The following is a *selection* of careers that may involve an interest in science, but should not be considered a comprehensive or complete list.

Legislators and Senior Management

0011   Legislators

0012   Senior Government Managers/Officials

0014   Senior Managers — Health, Education, Social and Community Services and Membership Organizations

0016   Senior Managers — Goods Production, Utilities, Transportation and Construction

0131   Telecommunication Managers

0211   Engineering Managers

0212   Architecture/Science Managers

0213   Information Systems and Data Processing Managers

0311   Health Care Managers

0312   Administrators in Post-Secondary Education and Vocational Training

0411 Government Managers in Health and Social Policy Development and Program Administration

0412 Government Managers in Economic Analysis, Policy Development and Program Administration

0413 Government Managers in Education Policy Development and Program Administration

0414 Other Managers in Public Administration

0511 Library, Archive, Museum and Art Gallery Managers

0631 Restaurant and Food Service Managers

0722 Maintenance Managers

0811 Primary Production Managers

0911 Manufacturing Managers

0912 Utilities Managers

Business and Finance Administration

1122 Professional Occupations in Business Services to Management

1243 Medical Secretaries

1421 Computer Operators

1454 Survey Interviewers and Statistical Clerks

Natural and Applied Science

2111 Physicists and Astronomers

2112 Chemists

2113 Geologists, Geochemists and Geophysicists

2114 Meteorologists

2115 Others Professional Occupations in Physical Sciences

2121 Biologists and Related Scientists

2122 Forestry Professionals

2123 Agricultural Representatives, Consultants and Specialists

2131 Civil Engineers

2132 Mechanical Engineers

2133 Electrical and Electronics Engineers

2134 Chemical Engineers

2141 Industrial and Manufacturing Engineers

2142 Metallurgical and Materials Engineers

2143 Mining Engineers

2144 Geological Engineers

2145 Petroleum Engineers

2146 Aerospace Engineers

2147 Computer Engineers

2148 Other Professional Engineers

2151 Architects

2152 Landscape Architects

2153 Urban and Land Use Planners

2154 Professional Land Surveyors

2211 Applied Chemical Technologists/Technicians

2212 Geological and Mineral Technologists/Technicians

2213 Meteorological Technicians

2221 Biological Technologists/Technicians

2222 Agricultural and Fish Products Inspectors

2223 Forestry Technologists/Technicians

2224   Conservation and Fishery Officer

2225   Landscape and Horticulture Technicians/Specialists

2231   Civil Engineering Technologists/Technicians

2232   Mechanical Engineering Technologists/Technicians

2233   Industrial Engineering and Manufacturing Technologists/Technicians

2241   Electrical/Electronics Engineering Technologists/Technicians

2242   Electronic Service Technicians

2243   Industrial Instrument Technicians and Mechanics

2244   Aircraft Mechanics, Technicians and Inspectors

2251   Architectural Technologists and Technicians

2252   Industrial Designers

2253   Drafting and Design Technologists/Technicians

2254   Survey Technologists/Technicians

2255   Mapping and Related Technologists and Technicians

2261   Non-Destructive Testers and Inspectors

2262   Engineering Inspectors and Regulatory Officers

2263   Inspectors in Public and Environmental Health and Occupational Health and Safety

Medicine and Dentistry

3111   Specialist Physicians

3112   Family Physicians

3113   Dentists

3114   Veterinarians

3121   Optometrists

3122 Chiropractors

3123 Other Professional Occupations in Health Diagnosing and Treating

3131 Pharmacists

3132 Dietitians and Nutritionists

3141 Audiologists/Speech-Language Pathologists

3142 Physiotherapists

3143 Occupational Therapists

3151 Head Nurses and Supervisors

3152 Registered Nurses

3211 Medical Laboratory Technologists/Pathologists Assistants

3212 Medical Laboratory Technicians

3213 Animal Health Technologists

3214 Respiratory Therapists/Clinical Perfusionist

3215 Medical Radiation Technologists

3216 Medical Sonographers

3217 Cardiology Technologists

3218 Electroencephalographic Technologists/Electromyography Technologists

3219 Other Medical Technologists

3221 Denturists

3222 Dental Hygienists/Therapists

3223 Dental Technicians

3231 Opticians

3232 Midwives, Natural Healing Practitioners

3233 Registered Nursing Assistants

3234 Ambulance Attendants and Paramedics

Social Science, Education, and Government

Service (also applies to this book's companion volume, *What You Can Do With an Arts Degree*)

4112   Lawyers and Quebec Notaries

4121   University Professors

4122   Post-Secondary Teaching Assistants/Research Assistants

4131   College and Other Vocational Instructors

4141   Secondary School Teachers

4142   Elementary/Kindergarten Teachers

4151   Psychologists

4161   Natural and Applied Science Policy Researchers, Consultants and Program Officers

4162   Economists and Economic Policy Researchers and Analysts

4163   Economic Development and Marketing Researchers, Consultants and Program Officers

4165   Health Policy Researchers, Consultants and Program Officers

4166   Education Policy Researchers, Consultants and Program Officers

4167   Recreation and Sports Program Supervisors

4168   Program Officers Unique to Governments

4216   Instructors — Other

5226   Other Technical Occupations in Motion Picture, Broadcasting and the Performing Arts

Sales and Service

6221   Technical Sales Specialists, Wholesale Trade

6441 Dental Assistants

6442 Dental Laboratory Bench Workers

6443 Nurse Aides and Orderlies

6444 Health Services — Other Aides and Assistants

6483 Pet Groomers and Animal Care Workers

6621 Elemental Medical/Hospital Assistants

Primary Industries

8211 Logging and Forestry Supervisors

8212 Mining and Quarrying Supervisors

8213 Supervisors, Oil and Gas Drilling and Service

Manufacturing and Processing

9211 Supervisors, Mineral and Metal Processing

9212 Supervisors, Petroleum, Gas, and Chemical
      Processing and Utilities

9213 Supervisors, Food, Beverage and Tobacco Processing

9214 Supervisors, Plastic and Rubber Products
      Manufacturing

9215 Supervisors, Forest Products Processing

9216 Supervisors, Textile Processing

9222 Supervisors, Electronics Manufacturing

9223 Supervisors, Electrical Products Manufacturing

9224 Supervisors, Furniture and Fixtures Manufacturing

9225 Supervisors, Fabric, Fur and Leather Products
      Manufacturing

9226 Supervisors, Other Mechanical and Metal Product Manufacturing

9231 Central Control and Process Operators, Mineral and Metal Processing

9415 Inspectors and Testers, Mineral and Metal Processing

9424 Water and Waste Plant Operators

INDEX